D1322735

I've Got Cancer, What's Your Excuse?

ANNE GILDEA

I've Got Cancer What's YOUR excuse?

A Journey through
Black Dog Days,
the Big C
and Laughter

HACHETTE
BOOKS
IRELAND

First published in Ireland in 2013 by
HACHETTE BOOKS IRELAND

10 9 8 7 6 5 4 3 2 1

Copyright © Anne Gildea 2013

The moral right of Anne Gildea to be identified as the author of this work has been asserted in accordance with the Copyright, Designs and Patents Act of 1988.

All rights reserved. No part of this publication may be reproduced, stored in a retrieval system, or transmitted in any form or by any means, electronic, mechanical, photocopying, recording, or otherwise, without the prior permission of both the copyright owner and the above publisher of this book.

A CIP catalogue record for this book is available from the British Library.

ISBN 978 1 4447 4343 2

Typeset in Palatino by redrattledesign.com

Printed and bound in Great Britain by
CPI Group (UK) Ltd, Croydon, CR0 4YY

Hachette Books Ireland policy is to use papers that are natural, renewable and recyclable products and made from wood grown in sustainable forests. The logging and manufacturing processes are expected to conform to the environmental regulations of the country of origin.

Hachette Books Ireland
8 Castlecourt Centre
Castleknock
Dublin 15, Ireland
A division of Hachette UK Ltd
338 Euston Road, London NW1 3BH
www.hachette.ie

For Winifred and Charles,
my parents

'Don't see it as losing a breast. See it as gaining the ability to fire long-range arrows.'

– Michelle Read, friend, playwright, comedienne, the night before my mastectomy.

Contents

Introduction		1
1.	I Have Cancer!	3
2.	Bog	10
3.	Pathology	25
4.	Belief	39
5.	Debatable Beginnings	61
6.	Period	69
7.	Life Happens	79
8.	A/C	95
9.	Positivity	107
10.	Hair Here	119
11.	Nuala	128
12.	I'm Every Woman	143
13.	A Taxol-ing Time	153
14.	Sex	164
15.	Death	197
16.	Eugoogly for a Tumour	216
17.	Lady Writer	219
18.	A Wait	229
19.	Breast Off	244
20.	An End	259
Acknowledgements		275
About the Author		278

Introduction

Cancer is like a stupidly big lottery win: you know it happens, but you're sure it'll never happen to you. That's what I thought. Until one thirty p.m. on Thursday, 7 July 2011, when a polite, quiet-voiced lady, who seemed to know what she was talking about, said, 'We're ninety-nine point nine per cent sure it's cancer.' And she was looking at me.

I soon discovered that it's commoner than I ever imagined. So much so that the question, when you get it, shouldn't be 'Why me?' but 'Why not me?' Makes sense: we're living longer, under stress, over-busy, being passively poisoned by the myriad toxic by-products of our way of life, we're living contrary to how we evolved to live, over millennia, as mammals. We've each trillions of cells. It takes just one to go bananas, and suddenly you're shaking hands with someone who's introducing themselves as your oncologist.

I was told I had breast cancer. Previously the most outrageous thing that had been said about my chest was that I had nipples you could hang wet duffel coats on. Now the quirky compliment was usurped by the harsh scientific information that one of my breasts had turned itself into a potential killer. It had become a medical specimen in need of urgent squashing, needling, scanning and scalpels.

The good news is that it's not necessarily the Grim Reaper of a disease it used to be. Well, not if you live in a first-world country with access to a first-rate medical system when it comes to dealing with it, as I do. Medical advances have made it more a chronic than terminal disease. Not that it doesn't kill, not that there weren't big question marks over how it would figure for me.

This book is a memoir: of cancer, of the life it entered, mine, and of how I dealt with it. It's personal, which is deeply uncomfortable and embarrassing for someone raised a Catholic in seventies rural west of Ireland. The focus on 'me' feels, frankly, like a sin, but I've let go a bit of the natural reticence because I wanted to leave a record of myself after the potential ramifications of having cancer hit home. That's my excuse, anyway.

And there was something else. As I went through treatment, I often felt my deepest feelings were different from those experienced by others around me. It's easy to presume, given the general talk of fighting cancer, battling and survivorship, that there is a generic response to its diagnosis. But just as the disease is not homogeneous, neither are the reactions it evokes.

Deep down, my gut reaction to it felt like a dirty secret.

1. I Have Cancer!

That July morning I'd cycled into the hospital on my own, expecting to have a benign cyst drained. I'd almost not bothered going, such was my dread of the needle and syringe I imagined would be involved. I'd no fear it was cancer: it wasn't a lump. It was just a swelling that had been growing steadily for several months. I'd been hoping it would disappear as spontaneously as it had arisen. It hadn't. Finally I'd gone to the doctor, and had ended up in the breast clinic.

At eight thirty the waiting area in the breast care clinic was already near full. It was in an annex off a corridor. The hard plastic seating faced a wall of windows that looked out onto a small enclosed courtyard where a weather-battered decorative sign at the base of an old tree said, 'Welcome'. Inside, on a television suspended from the ceiling, a man with a Brummie accent was telling a woman with a television voice that he'd no problem pimping his wife.

Leabharlanna Poibli Chathair Bhaile Átha Cliath
Dublin City Public Libraries

I sat under the television, the better to ignore it, flipped open a paper and hoped things wouldn't take too long. A glance around the room showed the sombre faces of worried women. I felt separate from their medical concerns, which must have been serious: they all had somebody accompanying them. Behind us, doors to the suite of rooms where attendees were clinically assessed opened and closed. Names were called, women went in and out.

'That should be nothing to worry about. It looks like a cyst,' the breast care nurse said, when my turn came. I'd popped my top off, was sitting on the examination couch, and we were waiting for the doctor. I nodded. If it needed draining, the needle was nothing to worry about, she was saying, when he entered.

He felt the swelling, said it wasn't a cyst because it was solid. He felt under my arm, found a lump there, murmured, 'This could be serious.' He left, returned with the consultant. She repeated the examination. A biopsy was ordered. But still I was oblivious to what 'serious' might mean. Even when the pain of the mammogram plates pressing on the swelling made me almost faint. And during the ultra sound examination, when the doctor kept asking her assistant to freeze and save images of breast and armpit, saying, 'There,' and 'There,' and marking the areas that were of interest with little virtual arrows. What was she seeing? What were those blurs on the black and white screen? Could I allow myself that question?

Then she raised the examination bed on which I lay, and performed the biopsy. Which I found shockingly invasive, unprepared as I was for the deep dull pains as the needles pressed time and again into my breast and my armpit, snapping hard, like a stapler, as tiny bits of tissue were removed. I ended up bandaged under my arm and over my breast, throbbing and sore, slightly humiliated, overwhelmed and reduced to tears. I called my sister to come and join me to wait for the results. We were among the last few left in the waiting room as a.m. segued into p.m.

Time we passed, laughing, drawing moustaches on all the women in the waiting-room magazines because, despite everything I had just gone through, cancer did not seem my issue. Finally, after an hour or two, we were summoned to the surgeon's office. She was seated at a desk, but to the side of it, so it didn't come between us. Una and I sat in chairs alongside her. There was also a breast care nurse, who perched herself informally against a table by the door. We were all close: the office was tiny.

The consultant's voice was soft and exuded female empathy. She said, straight out, that they were almost certain it was cancer. The air seemed to leave the room. The words hit me like a punch. My sister started to cry. I was wide-eyed with shock. So the big cyst was a big tumour. It was crazy that, after everything that had happened that day, those words were still utterly unexpected. Me? Cancer? Nobody puts those two things together.

'What's the time scale on this?' I asked eventually.

It looked like surgery, chemotherapy and radiation would be required, she said. The treatment would take nine months. Nine months! I was to return to the clinic on the following Tuesday for the results of the biopsy, though there was little doubt about the conclusion. More diagnostic tests were ordered, because it was clear the cancer had already spread to the armpit area. A jumble of concerns flashed into my mind: what about work, the mortgage, gig commitments? Would I end up broke or dead?

There wasn't much else for the surgeon or nurse to convey. I had to go, be alone, and allow the diagnosis to percolate until it settled in as my 'new normal'. That's what they call it in Internet cancer chatrooms, I was soon to discover: 'your new normal'. Bloods needed to be taken: this could be done on Tuesday, or now they offered. 'I'll do it now,' I said, with an urge to edge the inevitable onwards.

Next thing Una and I were out of that office, heading towards the haematology department. We got to a busy main corridor. Spontaneously we stopped, hugged each other and howled. Ongoing everyday hospital business buzzed by. We were now part of that business. I was numb with the implications, high on adrenalin. We stopped crying. I needed to cry more. No, I didn't. I had to tell those who needed to know, to spread the news. I have cancer! What a drama! No, it wasn't a drama, it was devastating. No, it wasn't devastating, it was exciting. What was going to happen? Come on, bring it all on. If it had to happen, let it happen quick sharp: the coming cascade of medical processes, the game of chance that was the outcome. How interesting! No, not interesting, fucking awful – I wanted to get away from the place, needed peace, space, time to process it.

'What do you want to do?' my sister asked, after the bloods.

'Drink,' I said. It seemed the only way to deal with the daft gravity of the situation. Whatever I was, I wasn't one to be sick. Now, without warning, I had cancer – it was ridiculous. Throw back some alcohol, that seemed the thing to do, to put the boot into the shock. We went on a pub crawl and got pissed.

A sleepless night followed. The swelling in my breast throbbed. Was I bad to have let it get so big? Why had I delayed going to the doctor? And was I dying right now? Three a.m., and alone as always, I couldn't lie in bed. I got up, had to get out. I took the lift from my small third-floor apartment down to the courtyard. I sat in the rain. It felt like a scene from a film. That song about feeling the rain on your skin, how no one else can feel it for you, played in my mind – 'Unwritten' by Natasha Bedingfield. I'm not even a Natasha Bedingfield fan, but such are the curve balls of cancer. I felt my pyjamas dampen. My body pulsed with pain where it had been spiked, twelve times in total, for the needle biopsies. I'd let the tumour get big. I sensed it literally growing now in my left breast, though that might just have been internal bleeding from all those blithering needles. The song was on a mental loop: The film cut to the wide dark of the sky, the slanting rain reflecting in the artificial lights of the courtyard. I might be dying. It could be curtains – imminently. Wow.

Buried underneath the shock, panic and drama, the undeniable truth was that, on some level, I felt relieved. Should I pipe up and say, 'Actually, when I think about it, this cancer seems biologically logical to me – me, as in all-of-me, head-history-heart, not just me as in the patient presenting with breast pathology. So, thanks very much, hospital chaps, for the offer of all the chemo, surgery, radiation you mentioned, but I think I'll let Nature run her wise course. 'Bye now.'

'You're just depressed,' would be the next diagnosis. And, yes, indeed, that would be correct. For as long as I can remember, depression has been an issue with me. I've loathed myself for it. Most of my fellow seven billion could justifiably scream in disbelief at the privileges and freedoms that were mine by accident of birth. *Moi*, typical first-world navel-gazer, no? Belly full, roof over the head, surrounded by shops stuffed full of a plethora of everything. But I had a sick head. Boo-hoo. The illness, or mood problem, or tendency to be a stick-in-the-mud, disgusted me as it sucked the life out of me. 'Pity about you,' my inner niggling voice said, throwing up images of emaciated stick-humans, the ludicrous violence of war, and that kind of thing. Even this sudden illness felt like one of privilege – breast cancer! Instantly I had access to the finest medical science, when kideens the third world over are still dying of mosquito bites, that inner imaginary voice reminded me. It was a combination of the west of Ireland and Catholicism rolled into one, a vernacular that cut me down to size, and left me riddled with guilt in every interjection. 'What have you done with your life at all, compared to people who've really done things with theirs?' it sniped. For eighteen months it had been riffing on that theme.

I hadn't had kids. Or 'paired off'. I'd never had the inclination to do either, but now I had reached the age at which both became unlikely, I felt an extra, unexpected moroseness about the passing of those things I had never wanted. I'd been a free spirit instead, a pursuer of the artistic goal, which had felt a brave and vital choice at twenty-one, but in hindsight a rather reckless spree now I was double that age. A jadedness had set in, and though I'd been successful enough in my work, I struggled to find the passion essential to fire me. Also, I was relatively poor, with all the attendant insecurities that entails. I was having a long 'My mother was right: I should have done something sensible' moment.

For eighteen months before cancer I was caught in a loop of negativity that intensified as I berated myself for being caught in a loop of negativity that intensified as I … I slogged on, determined to see it pass, like slow storm clouds or a skulking black mongrel. 'Get over yourself,' the niggling voice berated me. But I couldn't shake this thought: Life hurts too much. I want out.

And then I was told I had this extraordinary disease. A gift! A release! A time-out! An impetus! A thrilling ultimatum! An adventure! As well as being 'bad', it was all of those things. It exploded me out of the interior lethargy of despair into the externality of sudden, dramatic physical disease. I wasn't overly invested in the eventual outcome. So I wasn't afraid. Fear didn't come into it. If anything, the emotion was excitement. I was just intensely in the moment, for the first time in months. And that was good.

That was what it felt like, right then.

2. Bog

An American once told me that scientific research had shown that the rural west of Ireland is 'the Mecca of depression'. Perhaps that's true. Or perhaps he was just trying to convey his impression of the scintillating experience of knowing me – because that's where I'm from, where my forebears were born, Mayo and Sligo, and where I was raised. I grew up on my father's small farm, twenty miles inland from the Atlantic, twenty miles from Sligo city, three odd miles outside the nearest town, the kind of place you'd describe in terms of its relationship to other places, it being an easily missed mark on the map. 'It was very barren where I was raised,' goes a gag I wrote for stage, 'the kind of place where you opened the front door, and as far as the eye could see there were alcoholics.' The kind of place where nobody ever said, 'I love you.' They just implied it, by crying a lot when you died.

The land was flat, divided into myriad small yellow-green fields, sectioned by strips of hawthorn hedge and bedraggled lines of barbed wire. Beyond, it stretched away in streaks of brown, the hinterland of bog – a bleak landscape studded with clumps of rushes, hard grasses, white dots of bog cotton, slashed through by the yellow flowering of whin bush, and scored with scribbles of rutted old road. The kind of place a tourist board might celebrate as 'unique and unspoilt' but of which a lonely old local, facing into it for the umpteenth time, and it raining like vertical rivers, might simply comment, 'Ah, shite.'

Further on again, in the distance, the low bumps of blue mountains undulated all along the wide circle of visible horizon. Above, the sky was most often a bruised porridge of cloud that variously spat, dribbled and deluged. All was mucky when it was wet, which was often. Your wellies suctioned in the muck as you mucked down to get the cows for milking, driving them through mucky gaps, their hoofs and legs all mucked up. Or if you were above on the bog the turf dust turned to muck, plastering you. And you'd cycle home soaked from a day's work, the peat-blacked jeans stuck to your legs, your anorak to your back, and even the T-shirt beneath, all cold and heavy with sky piss.

Work was the focus of activity. Adult hobbies, for men, included talking about work, politics and the weather, in as much as they impinged on the work. And drinking. And, for the ladies, baking, sewing and knitting, which were, in other words, also work. There might also be the odd opportunity now and again of a get-together, for tea and a dance at a local 'social' in the school, or a Babycham and a waltz in a dancing pub. For children, the wide-open spaces offered ample opportunity to run around, imagining you were somewhere else entirely. And for everyone, man, woman, child, there was also Mass and all that. If the place were reduced to two rules, they'd be: work, and wear clean knickers when you go into the town in case you get knocked down.

If the land could talk, it would have said, 'What a traipse of dark history has passed over here, from heathen invader to those blighted by no potatoes, from British butcher to those racked with the grief of leaving for faraway elsewhere.' If it were to write itself as a two-word song, it'd be 'Oooh, boo-hoo.'

You'd wish sometimes, walking the fields and feeling the heaviness seep up through your feet, that a massive wham-bam would blast the bones of history out of the ground. That they might lodge in the clouds, be swept to the sea and lashed out into the Atlantic, not that you'd be wishing the fish cursed with the Gloom. But such was the atmosphere of the place, at times so oppressive that it seemed only a catastrophic exorcism would enable life there to continue happily. Or maybe that was just me.

The fields were dotted with isolated cottages, many housing bachelors. Men, alone all their lives, tending their land with no let-up in the drudgery. Year in and out, pulling calf out of cow, and milk from teat, lugging creamery can to creamery, their man hands hardened and worn, wrinkling with work till they returned to dust. It seemed a thankless, relentless, instinctive enslavement to their acres. There was a brand of tinned peas advertised on telly back then. 'Batchelors! Batchelors!' the jaunty theme song went, like a celebration of getting on in life, not being married – and eating processed peas. I could never figure it out, in relation to what I saw a 'bachelor' as being.

Similarly, stuff on telly, like the pictures of Ireland that accompanied the National Anthem played at the end of RTÉ television transmission every night, always seemed to turn the land into 'scenery'. Heavy history and a hard master were what it said to me.

I'd reasons not to be a fan. For sure the land was loved – I didn't need to read J. B. Keane's *The Field* to understand the lunatic pull of a few acres. The lure of it defined my formative life, and has tinted the background of all of it. It was why we ended up back in isolated rural west of Ireland in the first place.

I was born and spent the first few years of my life in Manchester, in the north of England. With my older brother, younger sister, Irish mother and father, we were just another ordinary family in early seventies urban Britain. A normal, content couple with three kids in a Mancunian red-brick semi, on a neighbourly street, school round the corner, nice park nearby, with swings and a roundabout. Then, the Irish government's Land Commission threatened compulsory purchase of 'the place' back in Ireland, as was its wont. They were going to legally take those few fallow fields and bit of bare bog that were rightfully my father's.

There was hard history behind his ownership. My father had laboured for years, from when he was a child, on that spread of earth. He was taken out of school early, labouring to enable siblings to go to boarding school and beyond. His right to the land was his thanks, in lieu of anyone actually saying the words. In his early twenties he'd left for England with nothing in his pocket, despite those long years of work, and he'd laboured hard there too, first in the farm fields of Lincolnshire, later as a foreman painter and decorator all over Britain The land was the redemption, the happy ending he could give that story, whenever. Meanwhile our life was contentedly in England.

Until, thanks to that Irish government agency, we were dragged back. Inhabiting the place was the only way to stave off the state's invasion. The decision to move was made before it was taken: the compulsory purchase and redistribution of my father's land among the neighbours was never going to happen. No matter that my brother and I were already in school, my mother's friends, sisters and familiar life all round her in Manchester, and that the bit of land for which we were giving everything up was, frankly, in the arsehole of nowhere.

'You don't get milk in school in Ireland,' a boy in my junior-school class in Manchester said on my last day. We were drinking the little glass bottles of milk every child got given at lunchtime in England back then. 'They make you drink hot orange instead.' Wherever he got that idea, orange cordial made with hot water was the yucky drink your mum sometimes made if you were sick. Hot orange? I've never forgotten how ominous it sounded.

Life was packed up, and we moved 'back' to Ireland – 'going back' was how it was put, though my siblings and I had never been there before. We had been perfectly happy on the other side of the Irish Sea. Then we sailed over it and weren't any more.

I was almost six when we made the move from Manchester. I thought we were relocating to Fairyland, that Ireland was all blue sky, emerald grass, rainbow, leprechaun and friendly cows. I thought 'Ireland' meant a cross between the BBC's *Camberwick Green*, Disney and Irish souvenir storybooks. None of the adults involved attempted to dispel this notion. As I stood in the cold muck, experiencing up close the smelly reality of 'cow', bending down to clump together sods of rough turf and being told this was 'work' for years to come, harsh reality bludgeoned home.

I missed Manchester, missed it down to the sound of traffic that lulled you to sleep at night. The night in Ireland was so silent it rang in your ears, the dead black of it so total it was like being in a vast closed coffin. The nearest thing to traffic was two to three cars passing each other, three miles away in the town.

The town: two streets, perpendicular to each other, a square and a few shops. Two that sold clothes were called 'draperies', their windows chock full of things like big jumpers, Bri-nylon nighties and work boots. Two chemists, called 'medical halls', stocked everything on the rural pharmaceutical spectrum, from fancy talc to cattle dose. There was a scattering of others that included a 'grocery' and a 'victualler's'.

Double-decker buses, traffic lights, shops round the corner where you got Black Jacks and Bazooka Gum;

the railway bridge at the end of the street, school with a gym, all sorts of equipment and instruments; *The Magic Roundabout*, crumpets, coloured Polos, my red scooter, which had to be left behind, Duncan, Vicky and John-Tom next door, the cat: everything about England that had been so real was now a dream.

And Ireland wasn't what I'd expected. But at least I was learning about contrast. You lived in one place and now you lived in another. What do you learn? That you preferred where you'd been – England, oh, England, the tears shed missing it, all the bedtimes crying to my mother, 'I want to go home.' But there was absolutely no going back. It was as if stubborn roots bloomed from my father's feet when we landed. Happy or not had nothing to do with it.

'I am English,' I told anyone who enquired about such matters for long after. Which was hilarious, given that my father's father had fought for Irish independence; his mother had been active in Cumann na mBan. He'd hidden from the Black and Tans for three days in a bog hole, he'd escaped from Sligo Gaol; she'd risked her life more than once, running messages. That's all I knew about their efforts in the War of Independence towards the creation of the modern Irish state. Nothing was ever said that might have helped me understand their motivation, courage, experience. I come from discreet people.

Once, when I was fourteen or fifteen, my school GAA football team got into some sort of inter-schools final. The principal decided that, rather than rent expensive coaches, the whole school, three hundred-odd pupils, would walk to the town where the match would take place, a few miles away. 'I'm not going,' I said.

'But you can't not go,' I was told.

'I have absolutely no interest in Irish football,' I reasoned, 'and I'm not going to walk to that match.' So I stayed alone in the school, a nun watching me, and I was the only person on any of the buses when they came to ferry the children home – a small mad assertion of power in the morass of those powerless years.

One positive aspect of that story, that such dogged stubbornness stood to me in the long struggle to earn a living as I do, as a writer/performer. And a negative aspect, that I was never one for the jingoism of tribe identity. It could have come in handy, when I was bobbing around alone in the big wide world, to have folks I might have turned to and said, 'Help, I'm one of you.'

Having the work ethic drummed in was another good thing about rural reality: how could you eat your tea in peace if you knew you hadn't earned it? If I'd lived in a city growing up, it'd all have been writing to *Jackie* magazine to find out how to do a snog, and shoplifting Spangles and mascara, all boys and bitchiness, discos and heavy petting. Farm life was wellies and cows, picking spuds, saving hay, doing turf and coping with muck.

There were loads of farm ads on telly back then, cures for sarcoptic mange mite, warbles, then SOS, 'Stamp out scour', products like Leo Red Dry Cow Injector, Systamex, Panacure SC, Ivomec and 'Cheno Unction. It's a quare name but great stuff.' Names that would mean nothing to an urbanite, but were the everyday poetry of those isolated on agrarian acres. It imbued your experience with relevance. A city person might know how to pet heavy, but did they know that 'scour' was calf diarrhoea? No, they did not. But you could visualise exactly what it was, when you heard the word on the telly, always, it seemed, just as you were sitting down to have your tea. Wasn't it a privilege to make acquaintance with expressions such as 'cocking a field of hay', 'They're above footing the tuft', and 'Will you go down the haggard and feed the hens?' Phrases verging on the archaic.

'Chuck, chuck, chuck, chuck.' There's me, pre-teen, in cast-off Crimplene flares from cousins in England, down the haggard, with a basin of Clarinda cattle feed that I'm chucking out for the chickens. I've long hair down to my waist, I'm overweight and my dream of being a child star at anything is eroding with the onward tick of time. 'Chuck, chuck, chuck,' I keep calling, and like lunatics the chickens come running, heads alert, silly little eyes darting, crazy legs awkward in sprint. They love this feed: it's a treat. It's chicken Tayto, I imagine. I love watching them go at the hard flakes of feed with their beaks, and after, the comic palaver of how they drink – head into their old pan of water, head back and up to swallow it, chicken glugs.

I might as well be on the moon, so far am I from the dreamed-of opportunity to be on TV's *Opportunity Knocks*. I imagine being interviewed by Gay Byrne on *The Late Late Show* about my success on that English show– explaining that I had to jet off to LA after, to do films, sing for big wigs, have my photo taken with the stars, all that kind of thing that happens when 'things take off'. Nobody thinks I've got a big head, which is the main thing. I get a big hand.

In lieu of my telly audience, I sing to the chickens – songs I make up, because I'm no good at remembering the ones off the radio. They ignore me.

I would eventually sing self-penned numbers, professionally, in the United States, but in New York rather than LA, and not as I had imagined. And I would eventually be interviewed on *The Late Late Show* by a host who was no longer Gay Byrne, though the conversation wasn't about dreamy youthful success but cancer.

Early on a summer morning, I'd often go over to a bachelor, Mick, to pick mushrooms in his front field because it was a gold mine for them. 'Mushrooms just pop up, complete, suddenly, overnight,' he'd tell me. He liked roaming around mushroom-hunting with me, our huge age difference nothing when we were faced with the delight of a surprisingly white clump. 'Here we are!' exclamations from Mick or me – like it was a game and we were winning. We'd carefully pluck those soft white fungi, with their baby pink fluted undersides, putting them into the plastic bag I'd have brought. I didn't eat mushrooms. 'Anne is great! She'll eat anything, not like the other pair,' my mother was always saying to other mums, when they were having the fussy-eaters conversation. I'd find it embarrassing if I was there with my siblings. They were both like twigs, and I could feel the other mothers in the conversation looking at me thinking, Yeah, I'd say she does eat anything all right – everything more like, the big lump of her.

'No.' I never got around to correcting my mother. 'Not anything. I don't like mushrooms or other stuff, things I haven't ever had, like the blubber I saw Eskimos chewing on a documentary.'

Later I'd look back on the fresh riches Mick and I were picking, and I'd marvel that nothing mushroomy I'd ever tasted could have been as delicious as those just-picked mushrooms I didn't taste.

Everything on the farm was repeated in an endless cycle: seed to crop; winter feed; bog cut, a bit of heat; a calf today, a stew tomorrow. Day in, season out, year over, the same life. You could see old farmers grow as steady and circumspect as Nature's slow turn. They'd become so accustomed to the ways of Nature they might have been hawthorn bushes, growing craggy in tandem with the land.

And you could see in all of that, the hardy landscape, the barely changing life, the people, a pure beauty. But it was hard.

When we returned to Ireland we moved into the old three-roomed cottage in which my father had been reared. The house had been derelict, felt so even after a lick of paint, and getting the electricity wired in. It was to be a temporary arrangement, while the Bungalow was built. Bungalows mushroomed all over the west in the seventies. There was a book, *Bungalow Bliss*, full of designs. Some extended to the front, some were straight across, but all were basically a variation on the same theme – a housing hooray, as the people of Ireland moved from damp cottages to these one-storey, multi-roomed, generic paeans to modernity.

Rural Ireland rolled into the future in bungalows. Flick through that book, and go through Connaught, you'll see it manifested all over. We moved into our father's bad cottage in November. He'd begin the new bungalow the following spring. That was the plan.

To build his own house was his life's ambition. He and my mother had chosen the design. Meanwhile, we lived without running water. There were only a couple of power points in the kitchen. It was cold, damp.

At school, the projected illustrations in the language class showed French cartoon people buying baguettes and asking *'Ou est la pharmacie?'* One of them, Monsieur Thibaud, *'Il est ingénieur'*, has a friend, Jacques. Jacques lands into Monsieur Thibaud's new apartment, saying *'Tiens, tu as une salle de bain, n'est-ce pas?'* as he's shown around. Which sounded like a pretty forward question, but maybe he just had issues in the waterworks department.

And then we practised that exchange: *'Anne, tu as une salle de bain?'*

'Mais oui!' was my answer. I was fourteen or fifteen at the time – oh, Lord, the mortification of such small situations. The truth was *non*. We had no bathroom because the planned bungalow had not been built. Instead of bungalow bliss, I was raised in a glorified shed. The shame of that dilapidated place was as intense as if I were the embodiment of its damp and mould, its lack of sanitation and basic decency. Rather than being shelter, it felt like something you'd want to shelter yourself from. The notion of home never came into it.

I'd use talc and cheap perfume to cover the mouldy smell

of my clothes. Oh, the banality of bad housing, relentlessly disgusting – it cast such a long shadow. I was raised in an unhappy damp shed, the experience of which felt like bad-news smoke signals blowing over me everywhere I went, ever after. Thank you, Arthur Guinness, the adult capacity to ignore disintegration, old hurt. Thank you, curse of the land, the fields, the bog, the past.

Thank God we lived out in the country, isolated, able to hide. Whatever happened in the thirteen years I lived there, the dominant theme was cover up, keep hidden, never let anyone knocking through the door. Never let anyone in. The four damp-dripping, crumbling walls of that hated house contained an unravelling of family: the void of silence between parents, shot through only by occasional argument; a father 'under the influence'; an uprooted mother paralysed by the turn of events; anything you might own mouldering away; any hope you might harbour eroded by the festering cold of that utterly unhomely place. There was the permanent lack of shelter, and the constant headaches, as if your young head was splitting with the pressure-cooker unhappiness of it all.

'Poor friends are best!' a visiting cousin, son of one of my father's brothers, once said. My siblings, he and I blushed in silent embarrassment at his lumpen attempt at camaraderie before he got back into his father's new Mercedes and returned to his entirely other life.

I begged my mother to take us back to England but, however ludicrous our circumstances in Sligo, she wouldn't leave for fear, she said, of risking our education.

Disempowerment: one of the strongest lessons learned from those years. Keep the head down until you can get out. The solution, the happy ending to this unfortunate interlude, lay in the future, at college in Dublin. I was good at school, though chaotic when it came to study. My siblings and I were entitled to maintenance grants and full fees. Each of us would eventually escape through study. Meanwhile, though the blankets were half the time damp, the only secure place was bed. Sleep was the saviour. I fell in love with sleep, endeavoured to make waking a dream, in the day cultivating the art of half-awake disconnection, absence from where I was.

I counted down the time until I could escape, sleep-walked through Leaving Cert year, crammed for the final exams in the cab of the tractor, got good enough results, and the college course I'd applied for. When finally I made the escape, the most exciting thing I recall about moving to Dublin wasn't the freedom, new people, intellectual challenge, autonomy, the possibility of sex or the sheer conglomerated bombardment of new experience on my teenage senses. No. It was simply this: having a bath in the flat I rented with three other girls. I hadn't had one in years. I still remember the occasion, saying casually, 'Oh, I think I'll have a bath!' to my new flatmates having tea in the kitchen, the add-on bathroom directly off it. I closed the door, filled the tub, and will never forget the sensation of easing into the luxurious mass of warm water, smiling at how amazing it felt, laughing at the decadence, the freedom, and feeling, as the water lapped my skin, the past wash off.

Of course, the past didn't disappear in one Dublin wash. It lived on long after as a downbeat thrum under everything that happened. There shouldn't have been a need to hide any more, but it was hard to ignore the drummed-in instinct to keep a distance – hard to suddenly become 100 per cent present, and impossible not to keep drowning in the unexpected bleakness that still enveloped everything.

Time, not miles, was the needed distance. And yet the first thing that came to mind when the word 'cancer' was mentioned decades later was an image of where I was raised, the old house, and two words: 'You win.'

3. Pathology

Shock. I was in shock for the first five days and nights after being diagnosed. That was the length of my wait before I returned to the hospital to meet the consultant surgeon again. I thought by then they'd have established all the pertinent stuff about the particular type of breast cancer I was harbouring. How virulent, how far gone, how common, or not, and how long I'd left, if it came to that. I'd thought they could glean most of what they needed to know from the biopsy samples they'd taken from my breast and armpit. I'd thought, if it were a death sentence, I would be handed the details that day. I barely slept, with the odd anticipation of what I might hear.

Then, the morning of the appointment – I'd never experienced anything like it, the sickening mixture of dread and excitement. You assume you've experienced your full range of emotional states by forty-five, but this went beyond anything that was familiar – the alertness, anxiety, exhaustion. I'd lain awake all night, watching the clock slowly drag round the hours, hearing each one bonged out by the bell of St Patrick's Cathedral across the road, adrenalin rising as rising time came round. Up too early, showering, trembling, avoiding the biopsy bruises on the bad breast, taking ages under the comfort of the wash of warm rain, soap and rinse, soap and rinse, washing away the dragging minutes until the appointed time, due back where it had begun. Brushing teeth three times, looking in the misted bathroom mirror and seeing an unfamiliarity there, dressing in slo-mo. I got my sister up: she had slept on my sofa, to be with me all the way. She had taken time off work. I felt lucky for her being there. Her face was strained; she looked tired. Both of us tense with anticipation.

We cycled together, through the morning traffic, to the hospital, strode back across the hospital concourse to the place where the crazy news had, a few days before, been delivered. What if now I was told it was game over? Would ambivalence be banished, that shadowy sense of wanting to die exposed as delusion when thrown against the stark reality of death being unavoidable?

As it came close to the appointed time, I was beginning to hyperventilate. I paced the waiting area to try to calm down. There were only a few other women there, probably, like me, waiting for their cancer pictures to be filled in. The appointment time came and passed. And then my name was called, we were going into the consultant's office, and everything was speeding up again, too fast. We sat.

'How have you been?' she asked. I couldn't stop trembling, could only shake my head as if to indicate 'not good'. 'We can confirm it's cancer,' she said. That was it. Five-day wait for those five words. Definite confirmation of what was already presumed known. 'Do you want to ask anything?' she offered, breaking the silence that followed.

So much for all the expectation, now I felt disappointed. I didn't know what to ask. 'What type?' was all I could come up with.

'Ductal,' was the answer. 'It's spread to the lymph nodes,' she added. At the time I'd no sense of the significance of that information. There was more she could have shared: I saw that later when I got copies of the initial diagnostic reports from the hospital freedom-of-information office. But there seemed to be an 'if it isn't asked, don't tell' policy, perhaps because a mind in shock can absorb only a little at a time. And some people don't want to know everything. And those who do, their desire soon becomes apparent. And they are appeased.

More detailed tests were required. They began that day, with the magnetic resonance imaging (MRI), a scanning process that uses magnetic fields and radio waves to produce very detailed images of a body's internal tissues. Later there was a bone scan, a CAT scan, ultra sounds of liver, ovaries, the other breast, another needle biopsy. Beside me, throughout those days, my sister, wanting me to be OK, the two of us so close it was almost as if she was going through it too. But she wasn't the one lying on those diagnostic tables, in the midst of the activity. It's so much worse to be the one waiting in the corridors. I was distracted by all the action, the technology, the engaging novelty. I felt like a dog unleashed in a universe of new smells. I enjoyed the other patients we met along the way too.

While waiting for the MRI in a busy little room, I recall a hospital in-patient being pushed in in a wheelchair to await his test alongside us. He was a frail elderly man, wisps of chaotic grey hair on his near bald head above a deeply weathered face that spoke perhaps of living on the street. The most of what he had on was a blue paper hospital gown, an indignity alongside the rest of us well covered in our day clothes. His spindly aged legs were naked, his worn feet in old slippers. 'They always come and get you just when the tea's coming,' he announced loudly, in a great north of England accent, to no one in particular.

A nurse came to fill out a questionnaire with him. He must have been nearly deaf. She had to shout to be heard, his personal medical history broadcast to the whole room. 'DIABETES. DO YOU HAVE DIABETES? DIABETES?'

No, we all learned, he did not.

'They always come and get you just when the tea's coming,' he told the room again, when she was done, and he was left on his own.

This chap and I were called through together, to the antechamber off which were the two MRI rooms. I was given a gown, and told to undress for the test. When prepared, we ended up sitting side by side, in matching blue gowns, silently waiting. A silence he broke with, 'They always come and get you just when the tea's coming.' I'd heard his line so many times by then it felt like a comedy sketch. What would be a good punch line? The technician popping their head out and quipping,

'And what makes it worse is that it's PG Tips'?

I thought it an odd concern, given the situation. I mentioned the exchange to the MRI technician when I went through. 'He was sitting up on his ward all morning waiting for two things – tea, and being brought down for his scan, and they both happened at the same time,' she explained. The Beckettian conundrums of the hapless hospital patient waiting for a cuppa they never get. I found her empathy with him impressive. It was a level of sensitivity I experienced time and again from the personnel in that hospital.

I found the palaver of the medical testing fascinating. An MRI machine is predominately composed of a large doughnut-shaped magnet. I was asked to lie face down on a plinth protruding from the front of this contraption. My breasts were positioned to hang in two bucket-like indentations. A cannula was pricked into a vein in the back of my hand and connected to a line for pumping in contrast agent that would highlight tissue during the procedure. When it was all set up, I was reversed into the machine's hole. I was given headphones for my ears, to distract me from the loud hammering of the mechanism. Something soothing or classical? No – it made me laugh. It was a radio station, a phone-in about the banking crisis. I was listening to the troubles of the nation while my mouth filled with the taste of metal from the liquid being issued to the vein, and the machine hammered and clunked, and the plinth seemed to shudder. A thoroughly odd experience, like being in an interactive sculpture called 'Heavy Industry – Noise and Taste, with Ambient

Sound of Credit Crunch'. I might have been experiencing a particularly well executed exhibit at the National College of Art and Design's summer final-year show, round the corner from where I live. From a purely aesthetic point of view, it was riveting. And that was what my mind focused on. As for what the images might reveal – I didn't wonder.

'What are you in for?' asked a woman seated with Una and me in the CAT-scan waiting area. I was slowly drinking a jug of orange-flavoured liquid, the contrast agent that had to be ingested before the scan and would highlight the internal tissues during the imaging process.

I told her I had just been diagnosed with breast cancer. 'Oh, don't worry, I've had that!' she chirped. 'I had to have both of them off *and* the womb out. They know what they're doing here. The care is magnificent.' She went on to tell us that the daughter had had the breast too, and the husband the prostate, and the grandson the liver, would you credit it? 'Our family gets cancer like other people get colds,' she concluded, sounding almost proud of it. I imagined a hypothetical family coat of arms for her, a tumour and crossed syringes. I didn't want my illness to be a badge of identity, but I could see how it might happen: it was all-consuming at that time. I'd scant experience of hospitals previously.

'Just do as the machine tells you,' the technician operating the CAT scanner said, when I was lying in it.

I'd another cannula in my vein, for additional contrast agent. The machine spoke: an electronic male American burr, quite appealing, in a huge-intimidating-medical-appliance kind of way. 'Breathe,' the voice said, while a large arch of machinery moved over me. 'Hold the breath. Exhale.' Funny if the voice went off script, I thought, if it whispered, 'Nice rack, by the way,' between takes. When the contrast agent was pumped in, there was a flush of heat right down my body and into my pants. Let's just say, with regard to that particular sensation, the machine was the cancer-scanning equivalent of Woody Allen's 'orgasmatron'.

The radiotracer for the bone scan was delivered by needle into the bloodstream. I had to wait a few hours for it to work its way through the system, before the imaging proceeded. The tracer leaves the body emitting low-level gamma rays, a first for me – or maybe not: I had often swum in the Irish Sea. Being in the machine was pure sci-fi. It was in a large white enclosed area, the remotely operated wide, flat imaging plate very slowly shifting down the body, while you lie prone on the machine's hard plinth, trying to honour the instruction 'Don't move.' Occasionally the plate trembled and pinged, like a shy robot. It was slightly claustrophobic when it came down close to your body. The odd machine, the stark, sterile room, the sci-fi unusualness put me in mind of those stories of Americans abducted by aliens, returning to tell the tale of being bodily analysed. Are they ever asked, 'And are you sure now y'all just weren't being tested in the hospital for metastatic cancer, Billy-Ray?'

Within four days I'd had all the additional scans. The diagnosis: I was lucky. Though the cancer showed as having spread to all three levels of breast-area lymph nodes, crucially there was no evidence it had gone further.

It wasn't, fortunately for me, stage four. My final diagnosis was that the cancer was stage three C, grade three, triple negative. That grade meant it was fast-growing. The 'triple negative' meant it didn't have receptors for oestrogen, progesterone or HER2, human growth hormone, which limited treatment options somewhat. There were multiple lesions throughout the breast: the lump that had alerted me to something going on was actually a confluence of small tumours. 'I can't save your breast. You'll have to have a mastectomy,' the surgeon told me, on 14 July. I didn't care, right then. There seemed something darkly apt in it, given I'd been so low.

Yet I was heartened when she added, 'You'll have a straight, neat scar.' I'd think of that later when, prior to surgery, I watched YouTube videos of rough surgeon men chopping into women's breasts, like they were lumpy meat, then sewing the sides of the empty breast pockets together, leaving the wound puckered and raised, like the top of a sack crudely stitched shut. I felt glad I didn't live in the Middle East. Or Russia.

The surgeon explained the immediate options to be considered: mastectomy first, the standard procedure, or a newer approach, neo-adjuvant chemotherapy, chemotherapy before surgery. The neo-adjuvant approach is employed to shrink tumours before surgery. Also, when it comes to analysing tissue after the surgery, the degree to which the cancer has responded to the chemo can be quantified – an important consideration given I had triple negative cancer, and chemotherapy was the only systemic treatment available.

'What are my percentage chances of survival?' I asked, before leaving her office.

'What's the point of looking at it that way?' she answered. 'If I told you it was seventy/thirty, then the question is are you one of the seventy or the thirty? Rest assured that we wouldn't be putting you through all this expensive treatment if we didn't believe it was worth it.'

Later, in response to a column I had written, a woman emailed: 'I worked out that I had an 81 per cent chance of survival, but as a friend said to me at the time, the reality is that it is either 0 or 100 per cent. Either you survive or you don't so the stats don't really matter – you can't be 81 per cent alive. So I dispensed with it after that.'

'Did she say how many liaisons?' Una asked, when we'd left the surgeon. We laughed until we cried at her malapropism.

Something someone who'd been through cancer said to me: 'Everyone needs that one person, the one who comes on the journey with you, who really shares it.' I can't imagine how hard it would have been if I hadn't had my sister Una.

I got a call the following morning, Friday, 15 July, at eight thirty. Could I come in and see the oncologist within the hour? Could I what? Whatever I am, I'm impatient. This was terrific. I had figured on a wait of at least a week while they decided what treatment route to take. Evidently they had decided on chemotherapy before the operation, and I'd be started ASAP. Another novelty to engage with, whatever else it was. I phoned my sister: 'Quick! I just got a call that we've to meet the oncologist now. It looks like we're having the chemo first.' We? That's the way we'd be talking about it, until the day Una used the phrase 'our cancer' and we had a reality check.

I ironed a shirt, pressed a pair of my best trousers, took time to do my makeup. Usually I never went near the iron: 'creased and crumpled' was part of my look, less a fashion statement than an expression of endemic, lifelong disorganisation. But I was determined always to look well turned out in the hospital. It was about holding status in interactions with medics. I loathed the notion I might be talked down to, and figured the clean-cut lines of a well-pressed lady would work better than the Worzel Gummidge look. Having cancer was doing wonders for my grooming. That day, in her speed to join me at the hospital, my sister had fallen out of bed and into any old clothes. Her hair was matted, unbrushed, and she was wearing a tatty old cycle jacket, her eyes still full of sleep, tired from all that had happened that week. Every medic we met that day addressed her first, assuming by her dishevelled appearance she must be the one 'going through it'.

The oncologist rushed in the door of his office. Una and I had already been shown to seats on the patient side of the desk. 'So, Anne,' he said to my sister.

'Hello.' I redirected his attention. He introduced himself by his first name. The informality surprised me because his brusque manner and general demeanour didn't immediately suggest it. I addressed him then and always as 'Doctor'.

He sat, clicked up my details on his computer, delivered

a surge of information in a matter-of-fact staccato: surgeon thinks tumour visibly growing; chemotherapy to commence next Wednesday, eight doses, fortnightly, four adriamycin cyclophosphamide. 'Sorry, could you spell that?' I interrupted. My sister was taking notes and I could see a bonkers spelling scrawled across the page. I wanted it to be correct: I'd be Googling the instant I hit home. He complied, then the speedy spiel continued. And four Taxol. Hair gone, all of it, end of week two. Periods would stop, most likely not to return, given age. 'Will I be able to keep working?' I asked, desperate to fish out some, whatever, additional information in what would be minimal face time with this pacy chap who was suddenly God of my immediate destiny.

'What do you do?'

'Write and perform with my comedy trio The Nualas.'

'Never heard of you.'

Soon I was popping my top off yet again, boobs akimbo in another surgical setting. I sat on the diagnostic bed, as he pressed my still smarting left breast all over, focusing on the swelling I'd seen fit to ignore for so long. Under his analytical touch even I could sense the startling mass of it; he felt around the soft ordinariness of the right breast to compare, and commented, 'It's big,' about the tumour. I'd discover he never minced his words. It was something, along with his brusque sense of humour and self-assured professionalism, that I would come to like him for. That day I found his manner crushing. He swept a piece of paper across his desk, saying, 'Sign this.' It was a declaration that I understood potential side effects of the chemotherapy programme he was about to oversee. Under a long typed list, he'd handwritten 'death'.

'Death?' I queried, shocked, yet almost laughing at the bluntness, the ridiculousness of it, as a 'side-effect'. Can it be deemed a mere 'side-effect'? One in two hundred, severe reaction, can happen, he clarified snappily. I signed. Appointment time to be made at Reception. See nurses across the hall for weigh-in and bloods. Lots of rubbish on the web – avoid. If you have to go there, recommended site: Macmillan.org. He scribbled out a prescription: list of medications to get at my pharmacy – don't forget to bring them along on Wednesday, the day of first chemotherapy. The nurses would explain then.

And that was it, boom-boom, choppy-chop, over and out. Reassurance I was embarking on a well-trodden path of the best-targeted treatment, a sense of the enormity of it, a sense of business as usual, a sense of being in the hands of a competent, if chippy-choppy, expert. 'I've a lot of other women to see,' was the answer to a final question I'd tried to shoe-horn in.

'I'm sorry,' I said.

'Don't be sorry,' he snappily replied, then answered whatever that question was. I've forgotten, but I recall the exchange and that I could have questioned him endlessly in the madness of trying to get a handle on what was happening. And in that context I retrospectively appreciated his no-nonsense manner – sort of.

Across the corridor, in the weighing and bloods room, I collapsed into a chair and howled. And I mean howled. Animal, from-the-gut distress. The meeting with the oncologist was the culmination of eight days of unexpected information and startling incident. In that moment I was suddenly overwhelmed by it all, it having been topped off with that avalanche of detail just dumped on us. 'Anne, we have to weigh you now,' a nurse said.

Eight days before, I'd come to this hospital thinking I was having a benign cyst drained. Then this, and this, and this, and this: a week of needles and scans and extraordinary meetings, the sense of my private person being thoroughly pricked, prodded and exposed in exploration of its internal tissues, the breast, a most private, vulnerable part of me, as privately, at home alone, through sleepless night after sleepless night, I attempted to assimilate the fact underpinning it all. I was so far from mentally processing it – and before my head could catch up, the poisoning of my body would commence. No words for the feeling of it, only that howl from my gut as, finally, I really cried. It just howled out. It was relief, distress, communication – and it had to be truncated.

'Anne, we have to weigh you now,' the nurse repeated, in a firm, gentle voice.

'Sorry, sorry, yes,' I said. It was a relief, too, to snap back into getting on with it, engaging with another medically necessary distraction: weighing in, and having blood taken.

Soon the nurse was delivering more bad news. Breast-cancer chemotherapy doesn't necessarily make you lose weight, the opposite in fact. You have to take steroids with chemo, to stop your body rejecting the poison, and they puff you up. And it's partly that we live in a 'when you're sick, eat' culture, the nurse warned. In her experience the average weight gain was eight to ten pounds. So, no fashionable emaciation then, the very least one might expect with a bout of cancer. I've always had issues with weight. If eight to ten pounds was 'the norm', for sure I was going to gain weight. Great. I'd end up looking like a one-titted Buddha.

In the months to come I flipped between finding the oncologist's brisk manner upsetting and reassuring. 'He's the best there is,' was the general consensus from other women I met in his care. One, who was a bit miffed, told me that when she'd completed the last leg of her treatment, radiotherapy, she'd asked him if she'd be getting more scans. No, he told her. She was done. 'But how will I know I'm cured?' she wanted to know.

'When you die of something else,' he'd answered.

A bit insensitive, I thought, when the alleged exchange was related to me. I was in the middle of chemo treatment. But later, having been through all the treatment, I thought his answer succinctly spot-on, and funny: yes, breast cancer is a whammy of a diagnosis, but it's treatable, mostly curable, and ultimately the outcome we fear, death, is a fate that awaits us all anyway.

'Do you want to live?'

Later, I wondered why that wasn't the first question the oncologist asked. There was a debt crisis and it's expensive treatment. Given that economics underpins everything now, isn't that a logical question? I would have answered, 'Can I get back to you on that?' Instead everything about that Speedy Gonzales of oncology suggested I was going to be OK: he was going to kill my cancer.

The life-or-death issue was a private one.

4. Belief

'Anne, I'll do all I can for you,' my mother said, 'which is pray.' She was on the phone from her home in England. 'Now I want you to do something for me.'

'Yes, Mum.'

'Go and get Padre Pio's Glove.'

She wanted me to visit the former glove of the late bilocating, stigmata-handed Catholic priest-saint. And do what? I wondered. 'Smell the glove', as in the title of the Spinal Tap album?

'They give it to you. Hold it to your breast,' she explained. She wanted me to find out where 'they' were (they were in Dublin apparently), and through divine intercession, via an item of old clothing, I would be, if not instantaneously cured, at least proactively doing something to help instigate that outcome.

So, on the one hand there was a formidable medical scientist, my oncologist, prescribing delicately modulated poison, with the statistically based expected outcome that the tumour and any of its microscopic offshoots would be well and truly trounced. Not to mention the planned surgery and radiation. And on the other hand there was my mum's suggestion: rub the suspect area with the ragged remains of a dead man's mitt.

My friend Sean said I should go the whole hog and get the scarf and hat to match. The healing winter set.

Holy medals, relics, prayer cards and notifications of novenas and masses offered came in the post, not just from religious relations but from readers of my newspaper column. Previously I might have been open to the idea that such good vibes could have a transformative effect. Now, I didn't feel any inclination to contemplate the extra-sensory. Getting something like the Big C often turns people on to the Big G. It didn't with me. Rather, I felt the last tendrils of my F wilt – FAITH.

My niece asked me, 'Annie, what's soul?'

'What's soul?' I said. 'Why, that's a beautiful question. Asking someone what's soul is a bit like asking a fish what's water. It's something we can only intuit, not comprehend. That's why we talk about belief in relation to soul. When we talk of the soul we talk of our connection to the great mystery of the boundless universe. And just as we say the soul is in the body, so we may say the body is in the soul. What I believe is that each one of us has a unique role to play in the unfolding drama of the universe, that each of us has a journey that far exceeds our brief sojourn on this planet and that to me is soul.'

And she said, 'Wow. So if that's soul, what's R&B?'

That was a joke I wrote, less for the jokiness really, more

to express the faith I then held. It was based on the idea of The Soul as expressed by Minister, Rev. Bill Darlison in a sermon one Sunday at the Dublin Unitarian Church, near where I live, at St Stephen's Green in Dublin. Another Sunday, in the mid-2000s, at that church, I heard a guest speaker, astrologer Courtney Roberts, preach: 'Meaning is as intrinsic as light, and meaning, along with time and space and gravity and mathematics, was encoded and exploded into the universe that blossomed with the Big Bang and each of us, you in particular, was meant to be there from the start.' At the time, that seemed startlingly well put, completely right and fitting to me. I longed for it to be so. My being intuited it to be true; it sounded like a maths of faith.

Then in the couple of *über*-gloomy years before the advent of cancer, I'd released my hold on such hopes, let them disintegrate in a supernova of *ennui*. So getting cancer was logical, those diffuse breast tumours the embodiment of where my head had been. In that regard, the disease was, oddly but undeniably, a relief.

If any salvation were to come, it would be from that medicine man in my local hospital, not the mumbo-jumbo, wibbly-wobbly thinking of 'There must be more to life'. It was easy to put my trust in the oncologist: not only did he come with the reputation of being the best, but I had the lightness of not really caring. At the very least, turning up at the hospital was something to do. Why not engage with the proffered medical activity? And, in the roll of the dice of that choice, survive another while? The formerly unhappy *ennui* was suddenly kind of delicious.

So, God didn't come into it. Actually, I'm reminded of a fellow chemo patient wryly commenting that our oncologist thought he was God. And so what if he did? You wouldn't want the prescriber of your poisons to come across as a self-doubting ditherer – 'So I thought we'd give the old A/C a shot and, fingers and toes crossed, hopefully you won't explode. Sure what do I know at the end of the day, what?'

Meanwhile, my mother was on the phone, entreating, 'Anne, please, don't forget your Faith.'

Catholicism! How could you ever, in fourteen billion years, having been reared into it, forget it? You didn't have to practise, or even believe any more, to react every day like a Catholic. Taught from as soon as you could be taught that you're nothing if not naughty, and you should try not to be, but you'll never succeed – the Catch-22 of being a Catholic human – who could ever forget such an astounding message? And even if you lapsed, just living in the ordinary flow of Ireland was reminder enough: 'sorry this' and 'sorry that', apology as a way of communicating; the national habit of having to ask a dozen times when offering anything, 'Ah, go on, you will' because you never know does 'no' mean 'no' or what. Because having the confidence knocked out of you from the year dot, as per Irish-Catholic tradition, makes you ever uneasy about articulating, or even knowing, what it is you feckin' want. And the guilt! The guilt over everything, for everything, ever after, to the point at which you hear a Garda siren on the street and your first instinct is to throw up your hands and shout, 'It was me, probably.' Not to mention the bong-bong-bong of the Angelus bells at midday and six on the National Broadcaster, on telly accompanied by a little film of two girls painting pictures of angels, really crap pictures, stunningly bad, it has to be said, even for eight- or nine-year-olds.

You couldn't 'forget' it for the long-ago thrills it gave too. Like First Confession, which at seven was less about catechism, more about being finally allowed into the confessional box – the piece of church furniture like a three-door wardrobe, more redolent of C. S. Lewis books and fantasy kingdoms than sin and forgiveness. It was so at odds with the humdrum of ordinary stuff that going into it felt like a fantastic game. The mad wow of it – entering, kneeling, the hatch sliding back, you saying, as taught, 'Bless me, Father, for I have sinned.'

And the lunatic complication about what was actually a 'sin'. 'Can you give us an example of sins, Father?' we asked the priest, before our First Confession.

'I stole some sugar,' he said, not realising that 'stealing sugar' wasn't high on a child's naughty agenda in the seventies. Maybe in the past, when stuff like 'And I coveted my neighbour's penny-farthing' might have been a consideration. My standard sins became 'I didn't do what I was told, and I said a bad word.' Whether or not I had didn't matter.

My siblings and I made our First Confession in the church adjacent to the school we attended, where my father's sister taught. It was miles from where we lived, not our home parish. Our local parish church, the one we attended with our parents, wasn't as fancy as that school church. One of the many extra ecclesiastical doo-dahs it didn't have was a proper open-the-door-and-go-in confessional box. Instead, for confessions, there was what you might call a kneely-partition. It was basically a varnished wooden panel, on a wooden stand, with a no-nonsense unadorned wooden plank of a kneeler at one side. There was a fancy hole cut out of the middle, at the height that the head of a kneeling average adult would reach. That's where you, the penitent, went. The priest sat the other side, positioned sideways, with his ear to the hole, his eyes looking away. But one gawk sideways and he could see clearly who you were. There was none of the cryptic gloom of the proper sinner's box, with the grille over the hatch between you and the father that meant he couldn't see who you were. Only, of course, they knew anyway by your voice. Such were the crosses to bear of living in the tight community.

Anyway, the confessional panel was set up in front of the altar, and the penitents lined up down the aisle, the top of the queue at a discreet enough distance so that whatever was passing between priest and kneeling parishioner wouldn't be overheard. This was no space for a revelatory confession to unfold with a priest, a getting-off-the-chest or a repenting breakdown: even if mumbled words couldn't be heard, everyone could read the body language. You were in full view of the queue, and the people in the pews rhyming through their penance, having already been at the kneeler.

That was my brother and me, one Saturday evening, watching the action at the confession panel, having finished confessing the 'said a bad word' and 'didn't do what we were told' usuals. We were nine and eight respectively. And our particular interest in the action at the panel was our younger sister, who had just been trained into confessions at the other church. How would she manage with this more basic set-up?

Una had slight hearing problems when she was a child so she tended to talk loudly. And, indeed, this was what she proceeded to do, her every word crisp and clear, echoing all over the otherwise dead silent church as if she were announcing, not confessing: 'Bless me, Father for I have sinned,' her little seven-year-old voice boomed. My brother and I choked with laughter, our hilarity ratcheted up by the need to keep it in, and increasing as her short litany of innocent sins unfolded. A child telling a grown man potty reasons why she was guilty was absurd enough. But hearing that monologue echo through a tiny country church, peopled with a queue of people pretending-to-close-their-ears-to-what-was-impossible-not-to-hear, was simply comedy de luxe. A comedy further compounded by the crackpot stance she took at the panel: instead of kneeling, perhaps fearing her little head wouldn't reach the confessing hole, she stood and hunched forward from the waist, hands on knees, and peered through the hole to the priest, as if he were a tiny man she was talking down to – some quirky fellow, a holy leprechaun, behind a piece of cut-out wood, who, by his positioning, made communication complicated so she was playing peek-a-boo with him. Her pose exploded the reverence of the Saturday-evening Roman Catholic sacrament, the memory one of the funniest we three share of our childhood.

Naturally Una wasn't laughing then or after – the only word for it from her perspective was 'humiliation'. And I remember too, at the time, beside the comedy of it, feeling protective of her, her little face a confusion of embarrassment as she returned to where Kevin and I sat. I felt angry that she'd been put in such an exposed situation, unprotected – an emotion that became a theme for the three of us throughout our growing-up. And as the elder, a sense of my role as protector of my little sister grew as we grew, became core to our relationship. Which is why, through the cancer, the role-reversal was a bit fraught for both of us. And why, too, when I look back on that memory, I want to step, as an adult, into the past, walk up to that altar, bring common sense, some mature sensibility, to the situation, and say, 'Stop. This isn't fair on the child, my sister.'

And she was so nice! Her favourite food was corn flakes. I remember her asking Santa to fly over Africa and drop boxes of Kellogg's for all the starving children there – we were always seeing them half dying on telly. 'Corn flakes for Africa' – the campaign in her heart for an end to world hunger.

There was no sacrament in our religion for celebrating what was intuitively lovely inside the human. You had to be bad. Why was that? I remember once, when I was eleven or so, having a go at addressing it head-on. A visiting 'trendy priest', presiding over our school-class confessions, decided he'd do it by sitting in a church pew rather than in the box, and you'd confess kneeling beside him. No wooden panels or grilles of church furniture at all between you, it was to be just an honest one-to-one between humans – albeit one of the humans was there on behalf of God. Well, I thought, if this is about honesty, I haven't really done anything wrong or bad since last confession, so that's what I'm going to say. It was an experiment in trying to be authentic. So that was what I told the priest. 'Bless me, Father, for I have sinned. Actually, I haven't sinned.'

And what did he do?

There was a pause, and then he insisted. 'There must be something.' Why couldn't he have said, 'OK, I hear you. I believe in the possibility that an eleven-year-old hasn't done anything that might be classified as sin since she last confessed an exceedingly short while ago.'

Disappointed, I fed him some lies, the sins I hadn't committed, the usual. Lies to access the forgiveness for what I hadn't done, with the usual three Hail Marys and two Our Fathers 'penance'. The lesson learned: in Catholic life being openly honest isn't necessarily the way to go, the truth isn't necessarily self-evident, and if you really, truly feel the urge to articulate what you find when you listen to your gut, you should probably think again.

Even the penance for the sins you didn't do was tosh. People in the Bible had to go wandering forty years in the desert as 'sorry'. Now, that's what you could call 'penance'. You'd do the equivalent of recite two short poems you didn't understand five times, kneeling in a sweet-smelling chapel? It was all fantastically bonkers.

Speaking of which, there were, too, the unforgettable dressing-up parades, otherwise known as Communion and Confirmation: rather than delight at finally getting to eat some Jesus, Communion was primarily, for the girlies especially, the thrill of the dress, the juvenile outing as mini-bride – mine was an ode to seventies nylon lace, a mini with a skirt of such a scrunched-up bunch of it that if I'd stood near a flame I'd have gone up like gelignite. Not to mention the accessories: sparkle-embossed veil, lacy gloves, little ridiculous bag, fancy white patent leather shoes that made your feet feel like they should be dancing. Shuffle shuffle, step hop, twist and Body and Blood of Christ, Amen. My aunt, the teacher, who lived over the road, had bought it all so I didn't feel up to asserting the notion that I'd have preferred a maxi and less mad lace. And maybe not a veil that reminded me so much of net curtain because, let's face it, my head wasn't a window, was it?

The next big day out, Confirmation, at the age of twelve, was a repeat of the outfit obsession: a new blue suit – sleeveless dress, bolero jacket – wedge sandals. I looked the absolute cutting edge of what my mother wanted me to wear, it being, in fairness, her purchase from money saved cycling round doing local 'home help'. She who pays the piper calls the tune, even if it's Crimplene. What was it with the ubiquity of that unnatural, scratchy fabric back then? A rough ould penance of a cloth, a would-be saint looking into extra ways of flagellation could have worn it as undies, and been assured of fast-tracking into the Kingdom of Heaven come death.

I remember this, too, of the day we bought the outfit in a drapery in Sligo: there was a front-page story on my father's English tabloid about people over there called 'punks', who, the photos showed, were half dressed in black ripped stuff, with safety pins and chains in their bad-skin faces and demonic wildness in their wide eyes and aggressive pointy hair. An ordinary English working man in the story said he'd kicked the screen of his telly in when the punks came on because he was so annoyed at seeing that disgusting rubbish in his own living room – which, come to think of it, was in itself a punk thing to do. Punk: those people weren't massively older than me; the image of them was challenging, unnerving. England had become a black-rubber and safety-pin scary place.

In Ireland, meanwhile, I was having my big blue-Crimplene day out. The day my age group of Catholics agreed, as nearly-grown-ups, that we were indeed Catholic for good. The ceremony involved kneeling in front of the diocesan bishop, the hierarchical VIP, the provincial A-lister, with his big pointy hat. At a certain point in the proceedings, apparently, he'd slap you across the face in a ceremonial manner. The looniness of that was something to look forward to. Plus you got to choose a new name for yourself, to honour the sort of 'baptism by your own volition' of the occasion. But, like everything, you knew you couldn't be too wild, or even true to yourself. You wouldn't be saying 'Tallulah' or 'Isadora', 'Chaka Khan' or 'Nora Sex Pistols, Your Excellency,' when the bishop asked what he should be calling you on this great day. Nope.

Especially not in my case, because my mother wanted me to take the confirmation name 'Bernadette' in honour of the saint associated with Lourdes. She'd been there once, in her twenties, helping push wheelchair-bound pilgrims into potentially miraculous troughs of blessed French water. There was the joke everyone told about the paralysed man being pushed into the Lourdes water, and still not being able to walk when he came out, but his wheelchair had new tyres. I disliked the name 'Bernadette': it reminded me of that gag, and that my mum's idea of best-holiday-ever was chanting rosaries and hoping for miracles on behalf of the paraplegic in France. Also, it was the feminine version of Bernard, a naff man's name that was also the name of a particularly big lump of a dog. And anyone called Bernadette, you didn't call them that but 'Bernie', which sounded like a symptom of a bad rash. There were multiple reasons it sounded ugly to me, yet I took it as my third because it mattered to my mother. And I was never much of a one for putting up a fight. I'd never be using the whole hog of the name anyway: Anne Marie Bernadette Gildea, my full name, a name so Catholic it couldn't be more so if I were called Mary Pope Confession Paedophile Cover-up Virgin.

The only outing my mother and I went on together when I lived in Sligo was when we took a bus to Knock one night for an after-dark ceremony. Ten miles away, Knock has been a place of pilgrimage since the Virgin Mary appeared there in 1879, allegedly. The Mother of God didn't say anything when she showed up, the story goes. So, thinking about it now, it's fantastically practical the way her message was interpreted: 'A basilica, that's what I want – like a big concrete UFO. And hundreds of B&Bs, offering the full Irish with eggs scrambled or fried. Stalls, loads of stalls, selling plastic knick-knacks, with the stamp of the heathen Orient, "Made in China". Lots of effigies of me, but not me looking Middle Eastern. No, me more like a holy teenager from Claremorris, wearing blue and white sheets. Stick a crown on my head that doubles as a bottle top, fill me with Mayo water, enhanced by the bless of a bishop. And chips, lots of chips, and facilities for making bun burgers. I see chip vans, the Pope and 1.6 million pilgrims a year. And, believe it or not, Believers, a full-size runway above in the bog, despite the fog – in case I decide to land into ye in a jet plane next time, what? See ya, wouldn't want to be ya.' Like all first-division places of pilgrimage, Knock can come across as excessively focused on the tourism and kitsch-souvenir end of things – especially if you don't have the Faith. I suppose I did back then.

Our local parish must have organised the trip because we wouldn't have had access to a bus otherwise. And my mother couldn't drive. At least it was an outing, a getaway from the house. There was Mass, and a candle-lit procession in the dark around the basilica, our candles stuck through little folded boxes that lit up like square lanterns in your hand. Hundreds of people mooching around a circular route *en masse*, holding flickering yellow lights, like hundreds of small hand-held stars igniting the dark Mayo summer night, intoning the rosary as we went. At the very least it was undeniably unusual. Beautiful, hearteningly communal, a magical *je ne sais quoi* in the bleakness of everything else. My mother told me it reminded her of Lourdes, of similar after-dark processions she had experienced there. I could see the appeal, and loved that she loved it.

Another Knock memory. The trip there in 1979, when the Pope came. I went with my father, brother and half a million other people. We had to trek through a colossal crowded field. Actually, it was less 'field', more prairie. We were corralled in roped-off enclosures, each signposted with large letters and numerals. Like pens for cattle at a ludicrously huge mart, herded in by stewards. There was an awful lot of waiting: John Paul II was coming from a mass in Galway, where he'd uttered the stunning nugget, 'Young people of Ireland, I love you,' and though there were only around three hundred thousand people in attendance at his Mass there, compared to the bigger gang gathered at Knock, Galway had pipped Knock as a high point, even before he landed, late.

The waiting around dissipated any big passions, and eventually when His Holiness landed in, and got up on the altar, he was so far away he might have been made of Lego. You couldn't really get wind of his holy mojo, being half a landscape away from where he stood. We went so that we could say, 'We were there,' I suppose, but it hardly felt like we were when we were. The big memory is of cracking open the flask of tea and having a sandwich in the middle of Mass. That was a first. Giving out the Communion took an age, given the masses. My father said we'd better not receive, given we'd had ham sandwiches during the consecration, or was it the homily? Who could tell? We couldn't really hear. So then the only thing was the anticipation of seeing JP II up close, when he did a tour of the field in the vehicle that had become almost as remarked upon as himself, the Popemobile. But the close encounter with the pontiff and his transport never happened, due to some undisclosed security issue. Instead, after another interminable wait, he just flew away and all we saw was his white waving sleeve at the window of the light aircraft. And that was it.

My revelation that day? I didn't like being one of thousands of people waving and left behind. I wanted to be cast in the glamour of the skies, not as an extra in a giant genuflection. I can't say what else I got from it, other than that it was probably the only day out the three of us had together ever, and we all got on great, away from the shite that was home. That in itself made it special, that we went pretending to be a 'together' family and, like wafer becoming 'Body', the ceremony of the occasion made it real. Though papal anticipation was dashed, I remember it as a happy pilgrimage, with the brother I loved and a father figure.

'I think I'm losing my faith, Father.' My brother told me he offered that in confessions when we were teenagers.

'And anything else?' the priest replied, as if he'd just had a bog-standard humdrum 'I had a bad thought and said "fuck"' session, not an admission of a young Catholic being on the cusp of apostasy. As if, actually, it was something he heard all the time, something to be expected, a trifle to a world-weary priest caught between the realpolitik of people and the arch palaver projected from the Vatican.

A teacher said that if you stopped believing in Catholicism, it wasn't that you'd believe in nothing but that you'd believe in anything. Yet Catholicism called for some pretty stretchy thinking, which could be said to extend into believe-anything territory. Not to mention the manner in which the Faith occasionally manifested, madly, and appeared plausible to many – for instance, a most extreme example, the Moving Statues. In the mid-eighties Ireland had an epidemic of them. They bled, they wept, they seeped milk. None of it was captured on camera. Not one of them ever did a full-on moon-dance across an altar, shouting, 'This one's for the doubters.' The Fellini-esque phenomenon was, as I recall, covered seriously enough on the television news, while some media commentators simultaneously reflected that to the wider world we must look like feckin' eejits.

I'd left home for college in Dublin in 1984, and automatically stopped going to Mass. I lapsed. Another teacher had once said that he'd been in Dublin and some fella with a drum and a half-shaved head, dressed in an orange sheet, had tried to give him a book about his beliefs. And he'd said, 'No, thank you, I have my own Faith.' And the message was, that was what we were to do if men in funny get-ups were ever to attempt to push their dogmatic literature on us. Just say, 'No. I'm lucky enough to have been born into the One True Faith. I'm going straight to Heaven and you're not.' (To paraphrase.)

So I was delighted when I met my first Hari Krishnas

in Grafton Street, and couldn't have been quicker to take the proffered book. Only to find the ideas in the *Bhagavad-Gita* even more muddy than the Faith teachings with which I was familiar. The pop-out difference was that their saints had a lot more arms, and the occasional head of an elephant.

It's not that lapsing from Catholicism leaves you open to believing anything because you've lost the One True Framework to understand the chaos of being: it's that having been imbued with such redolent imagery, story, symbol and ceremony, if you leave you can still appreciate how any human might want to embellish their mundane existence with a sense of the supra-natural. 'I am not alone,' is the nub of it; 'We are not alone', the shared comfort of it; 'There is more', the hopeful possibility, not to say deep intuition, of it.

Having lapsed from Catholicism, I found myself drawn to many things spiritual. I've stayed up all night at summer solstice in a pretty shitty tepee, drumming for world peace around a roaring wood fire. And when the shaman (a Dublin suburban one) leading the ceremony said, 'See the spirits in the flames?' I said, 'Indeed I do,' and, as far as I was concerned, I more or less did. I followed that with a sweat lodge, where I sat in a swimsuit, cross-legged, on eerily slimy bare muck earth, in the pitch dark, with a circle of total strangers, in a low-domed hut, heated to sauna-level by hot 'sacred' stones, after a twenty-four-hour fast, broken only with a couple of fruit shortcake biscuits I happened to find. When the shaman suggested we had entered the realm of archetypal womb, I got it, and later when he said, 'Do you see that spirit over the doorway?' indeed I did, kind of, too. And I kind of liked it, but it was a bit too earthy: I got dirty, then was eaten by midges in the wild Wicklow wood where we were, and I figured I was maybe more into things that involved fewer feathers and drums, less woodsmoke and more central heating and tea.

I attended a mind, soul and body conference where a chap offered to cleanse my 'etheric spine' with a crystal wand for the special price of thirty-five euro; and I was healed through Japanese *jyorei*, for ten minutes, and got acquainted with *chakra* dancing, original wounding theory, shamanic *qigong* and bibbily-bobbily inner-baby bonding – one of which is made up, but does it sound totally implausible? 'Practise being grateful five times per week over ten weeks and experience a twenty-five per cent increase in happiness,' someone in an 'Increase Your Happiness' workshop said, and I thought, How very bloody true, probably. Not that I had the self-discipline to follow up and do it.

I sat through an hour of a man who claimed Johnny Depp, Vanessa Redgrave and Ross Kemp as former voice clients sharing what he'd evolved his voice-tutoring into: his very own 'Alchemy of Voice' philosophy. He had fabulous things to say about 'sonic mediation', 'feeling your note and reinforcing that vibration' and 'getting back to soul'. I get you, I was thinking, until the lecture evolved into an explanation of how the alchemy had been given him by twelve Angels of Atlantis who had appeared in 1987: an angelic communion from the fifth and seventh dimensions, somehow related to the fact that the Dominican Republic is an escarpment of Atlantis, and he was actually an alchemist and the planet is a cosmic experiment and our thoughts create reality, but that was quantum physics, and too complicated for the day that was in it. The intimation was that we were in the presence of alchemic speech-coach genius. My interest segued into the fascination of being in the presence of a probable madman.

I engaged, too, with the notion that there's an energy route to finding your soul mate. You think of three positive words about yourself, meditate on embodying them, project that energy into the world and find your energy match. I resolved to change my three inner words from 'late', 'worried' and 'headachy' to 'sizzling', 'fabulous' and 'zipadeedoodaa'. Then I forgot.

I've had tarot readings, fortune-telling, my tea leaves and coffee grounds read, and found nubs of true interest in all of them. More than one clairvoyant has told me the spirit of my maternal grandmother is by my side, which I have really believed. When I received an email from a friend alerting me to a prophecy of the Arizona Hopi Nation – 'The time of the lone wolf is over. Gather yourselves! Banish the word struggle from your attitude and your vocabulary. All that we do now must be done in a sacred manner and in celebration. We are the ones we've been waiting for' – it made such sense. Like: we're shifting from the Piscean age of the fish, of the two-thousand-year cycle of Christianity, to the age of Aquarius, which, whatever it will be and when exactly it will start, will be excitingly better. Yippee! The sense of things being made better seemed to underpin everything alternative-healing/spiritual I spun into, from Buddhism to transcendental meditation, EFT (emotional freedom technique) to a woman I knew who said she was doing *reiki* via the angels – I was lying in on a special bench in her house and she was invading my personal space with her palms while talking to shiny people with wings who weren't there. Whatever – it was the spiritual motifs of universal energy, connection, light, love, kindness, intuition and mystery, plus the endless promise of betterment, that I found endlessly appealing: each and all I appreciated as potential torch lights that might illuminate ways through the recurrent dark of life.

I lost that going through cancer. I was only open to the cannula for chemo going into a vein in the back of my hand every two weeks, eight times, and the surgical intervention that had to follow, and the radiation. I couldn't bear to hear a single mention of positive energy.

Someone sent me an email about positive thinking and getting better. They suggested a workshop called 'Heal-thy self'. What is this? I thought. You get cancer, people think you've suddenly sprung an interest in made-up etymology?

'I'm sensitive to energies,' an allegedly specialist masseur I saw before chemo told me, insensitive to my state of mind, 'and I sense your cancer has to do with regret.'

'All I'm regretting is that I ever darkened your doorway. Shove that up your gaping *chakra*s,' I didn't say. Anger's not great in the ol' cancer situation.

I received an email from a reader directing me to healing music on YouTube: 'The frequency of this Celestial Music communicates with the Divine Intelligence of the body at a cellular level raising the consciousness of each cell … The music resonates with an additional blessing for everyone who is dealing with any form of cancer,' went the shtick of the message, continuing, in a splurge of fantastic info: 'This May, as we each slept at night, our I AM Presence escorted us into Beloved Mother Mary's Temple of the Immaculate Heart in the Inner Planes. Within her focus of Light, Mother Mary helped our I AM Presence to expand the Threefold Flame in our heart to its original intensity …' And on and on in a spew of what seemed to me craziness. I checked out the music. It was less music than the sound an angels-and-aromatherapy aficionado might make while deluding themselves about their ability on a keyboard synthesiser. It made me angry.

Out of habit, I always cast an eye over Susan Miller's monthly forecasts on her Astrology Zone Internet site. A gay guy friend told me that Susan had once said, under his star sign, 'You have to go out this particular night. It's the best night of your life for meeting a partner.' But his only invite was to a lesbian party, which he attended. There was only one other guy there. They've been together ever after. And there's more: that boyfriend had been a guy I'd coveted in spinning class at the gym. Amazing! Wow! I used to think. Not any more, in Cancerville. Yet I read: 'Now, in terms of your career, 7 July is due to be a spectacular day, so special I took time to write about it in my "Year Ahead 2011" … On this day Jupiter, the giver of gifts and luck, will send a beam to Pluto, planet of power and financial gain. Whenever these two planets are together in a positive link up, as they will be on 7 July, it spells success. Pluto is now in your eleventh house, ruling community, social networks, charities, humanitarian efforts, clubs, and also your friends. Somehow these areas listed will be linked to the breakthrough you may experience on this day.'

That was her astrological prognosis for my star sign, Pisces, on the very day I was diagnosed with cancer. More to the point, I'd end up thinking she'd been, ultimately, absolutely right.

Meanwhile hospital poisoning meant I didn't have to do anything but show up. I didn't have to think. Or believe. I could just be. There was something rather pleasant about that.

I never did make it to the Glove.

5. Debatable Beginnings

The old habit of perusing the stars was tied to the fact that, from the year dot, I wanted to make a daydream reality: I wanted to be in the business they call show. Now, say you knew you wanted to be a top breast-cancer surgeon, the process you'd engage in would be logical: you'd get the head down, study your hole off, get the forty-seven A1 grades you need to get into medical school, then get the head down again, study your hole off, graduate with distinctions, start specialising in chests and cancers, study your hole off, work your way up the hospital ladder, studying your hole off the whole time, and in general, carry on studying your hole off, ever after, to keep up with the ever-advancing technical advancements, while of course being dedicated to your career to the point where it's less 'work for a wage', more 'vocation' on the life-or-death battlefront of cancer. Thus you get to, and stay at, the top of the medical science of which you are now master. Congratulations.

As a youngster I had that kind of desire to devote my life to something all-encompassing, but it was coupled with an airy-fairy goal: to be a singer, an actress, a person with the mic on stage or telly or whatever – anything of that ilk. That was the dream. I was willing to work me hole off too, but how, specifically? What did you actually need to do? I had no idea at all. So, in lieu of any practical methodology towards becoming 'a star', I read 'the stars'. Can you imagine going to your breast-cancer surgeon, and she says, 'Hang on a minute, just reading my astrological prediction in *OK!* magazine. It says my moon is retrograde, and don't be making any big decision for the next while. Now, about your mastectomy tomorrow …'

Nope. But if, like me, you didn't have a clue what you were doing, at least astrology represented some wacky pointer on a road that was otherwise without signage. Pisces: a watery, dreamy sign, very arty, intuitive, loves to love, a bit dribbly. That was the nub of what astrology said about mine. Which gave me the glimmer of hope that maybe if I dribbled around intuitively, true to my nature, the planets would see to it that I'd eventually find myself flowing into the dream. Silly? Yes. But also a tentative means of clinging to the flighty ideal, the thought that almost dare not speak its name: that one day the Super Trouper lights were going to find me.

Practically, growing up, it seemed our family lived too far from anywhere that mattered to ever make that happen. I did what I could, but pretending a twig on a lower branch of the 'fairy tree' on our farm was a microphone, and by talking into it I could commune with the 'little people' below to help with 'the dream' was, I knew, even at ages nine to twelve, an act of desperate 'proactivity'. There was no precedent for showbiz where we lived. OK, there was the bit of amateur dramatics in the local town, but at a three mile distance, it might as well have been Siberia for all that I, as a child, could surmount those miles to get involved. And there was always a local-joker type who'd be known for doing a jaunty turn at a parish concert, but his aspirations never went beyond raising the odd laugh the odd time while, more importantly, keeping the cows milked, the hay made, himself to himself and his dreams self-contained, in the instinctive rural way.

And there was always them with the great voice who could be badgered into honking out a song that could still a room by its rendition. And, given half a chance, with the sheer tone and musicality of their voice, they might have been a Bing Crosby – as I always thought when I heard my father sing – but the point was, they weren't, and they themselves never considered that they could be. Or if they did, they never had the chutzpah to do anything about it. So nothing around me could point the way to 'the top', which was where, from what I gathered off the telly, someone with showbiz ambitions ought to aspire to be. 'The top' in acting was for people with posh voices in cities; in comedy it was for rugged-faced Englishmen, Benny Hill, Les Dawson, Tommy Cooper and Dick Emery. And singing was for people on telly, delicately holding those seventies microphones that looked like silver sticks of seaside rock, people with starry names like Tina, Lena,

Nana, Dana, or Joe Cuddy, who'd made it somehow through whatever hoops and past whatever closed doors onto the box and into the posterity of professional fame. Meanwhile, the best I could do was sing into a hairbrush at home, or belt out the hymns loud at Mass and hope somebody's visiting relative from America or Birmingham was an impresario, and would be dead impressed, and whisk me off to stardom. Naturally that never happened. But the stars seemed to suggest that I should never give up hope because maybe some unprecedented orbs might spin across my sign in a once-in-a-millennium celestial conjugation and, wham-bam, the universe had its beams set on me. Maybe.

In the secondary-school convent I attended, the emphasis was on being sensible and realistic – whatever glimmer of talent or aspiration you might harbour in the showbiz direction didn't matter half as much as knowing the biography of Peig Sayers backwards in Irish, the life cycle of sarcoptic mange mite inside out, and all sorts of theorems, tables, laws, geographic and historic occurrences that would go in the one ear and out the other, once the Leaving Cert examination was done. That school's education was focused on the one thing: exam results. Exam results were for the one thing: a job. A job was about the one thing: the wage. If you were bright you might manage a great wage; if you were clever you'd make sure there was a pension attached. That was the *raison d'être* of the whole shebang: the pension/wage Holy Grail.

But in the convent, an unexpected performing opportunity arose. Debating. You could write a speech, get up in front of people and perform. It was hardly Broadway, the West End, or even Tops of the Town, but there was a stage, and a mic (sometimes), and eventually I realised you could have any old craic you wanted with what you were saying. Language was elastic, and the way you might say something could bounce multiple meanings out of it. And all the better if the meaning you intended was 'this is supposed to be funny' – and the audience's laughter told you they'd got it. Debating was encouraged, because it involved composition and structuring of an argument, and that'd stand to you in an exam, and exams …

There was no singing, dancing, feathers, slap or particular magic of make-believe involved, but a stage was a stage, and it was better than a kick in the teeth. Plus it had the added frisson of inter-schools competition, the glamour of a rented mini-bus taking you and debating supporters to schools up to thirty miles away, time out from the head-wrecking tedium of class – going on tour, as it were. So I eked out a niche as a debater.

When it came time to move on to college my main concern was escape from Sligo, not 'the big fat future career' *per se*. It was non-negotiable with my mother that, whatever the study, it would be academic. There were no third-level acting or performance courses in Ireland at that time to distract me anyway. So my main criterion was getting away to Dublin, the Big Smoke of Ireland.

My mother had amassed a heap of college prospectuses for my brother. He was a year ahead of me in school, and of much the same 'just escape' mind-set about study options. Browsing through my mother's library of college courses, I found a funky new degree subject called Communications Studies at the then newish Dublin City University. I decided that was what I'd go for: it sounded arty and cutting edge, the exam points to get into it were high enough, so it had the necessary 'academic' veneer, and, most delightfully, it was pretty non-committal in terms of 'What are you actually going to do, for work, in the future?' There was a smattering of linguistics, economics, a dash of radio and television production, photography, instruction in deconstruction, graphics, a bit of philosophy – you could study for three years, earn a degree, 'be qualified', if not in anything as such. I didn't dare dream that I'd ever have access to doing things for a living onstage, but to study the media-focused plethora of 'communications' at least made me feel like I was keeping my options open and sort of in the right direction. 'This looks interesting,' I said, to my still-fustering-about-what-he should-do brother. 'I'm going to apply for it next year,' I told him.

He looked at the prospectus outline, concurred with my enthusiasm, and went for it himself. So it happened that my brother and I took the very same degree, in the very same college, he one year ahead of me.

My brother was a speaker too, and from what he shared with me of his first-year college experience, I figured that establishing myself as a debater was a way to armour myself with an instant college-identity – the funny performer. I felt pretty sure I was good and unique enough at it to make a splash, so before I'd even set foot in the university I was going to, I'd set my sights on winning the freshers' (first-year students) debating competition.

I didn't win. A boy in my class did. He went on to the inter-university competition final. It was held in a huge packed pit of a lecture hall in University College Dublin. It was the spring of 1985: I recall him taking the podium, and I wished it was me. In a voice that suggested a struggle not to cry, he said he'd mistakenly been given the wrong topic for the debate. After an almost too-long dramatic pause, he revealed that topic: 'That Ireland is a fish.' He proceeded to argue against, saying, for example, 'You never heard of anyone going into a takeaway and asking for two Irelands and chips.' His controlled audacity ripped up the place: cheers, clapping, roars of laughter filled the theatre. He was the later-to-be-famous Ardal O'Hanlon. It certainly wasn't clear to me back then that such nuanced skill as he exhibited that night might lead to something as mature as a 'career'.

There wasn't a club comedy scene in Ireland at the time, no precedent for a 'profession' that could encapsulate such talents. Later Ardal, another chap in our class, Barry Murphy, and my brother, Kevin Gildea, would go on to establish the Comedy Cellar when they left college, the tiny club in the upstairs room of the International Bar on Wicklow Street, Dublin, that became the legendary seedbed of new Irish comedy.

Meanwhile, back in UCD that night in 1985, I was riveted and inspired. Writing and performing speeches ended up being the activity I was most consistently involved with in college. Naturally it wasn't clear to me then that that was the pointer to the path I'd eventually tread as a real-life 'profession': being and, even better, earning a living as a writer/performer.

6. Period

The weekend before chemo started I was in Cork doing a comedy festival with The Nualas. It was an outdoor event, with most established Irish comics on the bill. It could have been called 'The Does Anybody Know What's Going On Fest'. It was a mess. Acts ended up juggling instructions, like 'Instead of doing forty-five minutes at seven thirty p.m. tomorrow, can you do ten minutes in five minutes now?' I recall us arriving at our Portakabin dressing room and actor Frank Kelly, in the full regalia of his 'drink, feck, arse' Father Jack character from the sitcom *Father Ted*, popping his head out of the cabin opposite, enquiring, in his polite actor voice that was deliciously contrary to his get-up, 'Does anyone know what's going on?' Nobody did. It felt fateful, the kerfuffle and oddity of the whole thing, like life imitating recent medical history.

And then, in a scenario as silly as being moved to tears by mouthwash, or bawling about antiperspirant deodorant, I ended up sobbing over the sanitary products in Boots on St Patrick's Street. My period had started. I went to get tampons. One minute I was searching for the ladies' sanitary section, the next I was weeping, leaning against the shelves of Always Ultra and Tampax. The thought, This'll be the last time, was strong and upsetting. All the aisles of all this feminine stuff, everywhere the world over would suddenly, and evermore, be irrelevant to me after chemo; all those ads showing women sky-diving, horse-riding, running down the road in skimpy shorts knowing their pants were safe were no longer aimed at the chick I was to become; all those silly gags I'd written long ago, purely because comic convention said a comedienne referring to anything about her monthly biology was no-go so naturally that was what I had to write about, were now obsolete.

'I used to suffer from terrible pre-menstrual syndrome,' I used to say. 'A whole three weeks coming up to my period I'd be snappy and irritable. Then a week after I'd have even worse post-menstrual syndrome. In the end I went to my doctor and said, "What's wrong with me? My whole life is just one huge menstrual syndrome." He checked me over and he said, "Actually, Anne, you'll be pleased to know there's nothing wrong with you. You're just a moody old bitch, that's all."'

There always seemed to me something fundamentally comic about the shocking earthiness and animality of menstruation, the catastrophe of bright red suddenly on your white knickers, the shame and befuddlement that might ensue with its onset. I recall a supposedly informative booklet my mother gave me, purchased on that pilgrimage to Knock, called *My Dear Daughter*. It dealt with the new mysteries of the pubescent lady-body from a Vatican perspective. 'Don't be ashamed!' is all I recall from its instructions, in relation to the necessity of being hygienic with 'the hidden folds' of your lady-bits now you were menstruating: 'The hidden folds' suggestive of the mystery land of your down-belows, a veritable Narnia in your knickers. The 'don't be' suggested you kind of should be.

My mum gave me a packet of the mini-mattresses that were sanitary towels – 'STs', she used to call them. An ST was an oblong of thick, compressed cotton wool, covered in fine net, with a loop at either end that attached to a belt worn around the waist. The ST belt was made of a white elastic that quickly turned grey, with plastic hooks hanging front and back. Like a comic most unerotic reinterpretation of a suspender belt. Wearing one was like being back in nappies, or made you feel, under your clothes, like you were channelling a sumo wrestler.

Once, after a gig, a woman told me an anecdote of her sister having her first period, a family legend. The sister went to the mother, upset at the sudden appearance of this shocking blood. She was given an ST and told, 'Go on upstairs. You know what to do.' The girl nodded. She was gone a long while. The mother went to check she was OK. She found her lying on her back on the parents' bed, limbs akimbo in attempted relaxation, the pad, dampened with cold water, laid on her forehead. Such were the late seventies, early eighties in Ireland.

In 1979, I was thirteen, and a friend told me she was using tampons, which seemed brave and sophisticated. I wanted to, too. But I worried: could it get lost 'up there'? What if you put it in and couldn't get it out? What about that disease you could get from them, where one minute you felt like you had a cold and the next you were dead? And then autopsy revealed the mortifying truth: death by tampon. My mother was of the opinion they made you lose your virginity. 'Tampoons', she called them, as in rhymes with 'pontoon'. Later, at college, I recall a lecturer telling us that when they first became available in Ireland, bishops had given a Catholic ruling on the matter: they were OK, as long as the woman concerned exhibited self-control. Women were so pleasure-prone they might irresistibly find themselves riding their Tampax? The temptation to be a menstrual Jezebel trumped period cramps? Opening the possibility of choosing an uncomplicated relationship with a sanitary product over man and marriage? Amazingly, as with everything religion taught about one's sexuality, the notion of emotional context was entirely absent.

Eventually my mother bought me some Lil-Lets. There was fear and daring in reading the enclosed instruction leaflet, and going the whole way, becoming a tampon-user. 'I remember the first time I tried tampons. I just plugged it straight in, without reading the instruction leaflet. Afterwards, when I looked at it, I thought, Oh, no. I've done it wrong. I was supposed to slice myself in half first.' Another redundant joke.

Fear of the Tampoon was followed quickly by

revelation: it couldn't get lost! Your inner lady space wasn't a boundless mystery vortex your Tampoon might get sucked into, requiring the embarrassment of having to alert some outside professional to go in after it. No, your body stopped up there, eventually. You became acquainted with your own physical boundaries. Your inner being as a woman was demystified. In that regard, Tampoons were empowering. Was that possibly the nub of the bishops' issue?

End of periods, or period periods, as you might say if you were American: I met women delighted with that side-effect of chemo. They didn't see anything sad about being relieved of the monthly 'curse'. But I had never seen it as a curse. I read somewhere that the idea of calling it 'the curse' may come from the Irish *cúrsaí*, referring to cyclical events – a notion devoid of that taint of negativity. I wanted to remain part of the cycle, not have to deal with post-fecund-woman reality, whatever that might mean.

Would I miss former scares, the waves of relief when I wasn't pregnant? Was it that I was still 'planning a family at some stage in the future', at forty-five? No and no. The end of the eggs was nigh anyway; it was just the sudden finality of it, having to process that with having cancer, starting chemo, losing hair, losing a breast, losing God knows what else in all the rest of it.

Wham-bam, end of that massive aspect of being a lady: fertility. End of all my 'I can have babies' gags too. Wouldn't it be great if we could just lay eggs like chickens? Then you'd just have the one clear-cut decision: oops, look, I've laid an egg, should I hatch a baby, or do

I fancy an omelette? Or – a personal fave. I met a guy I'd known at secondary school, and hadn't seen for ages. In the course of our conversation he asked, 'And have you had kids, yet?'

Yet? 'No,' I said. 'Have you had prostate cancer yet?'

That was based on an actual exchange, not that I asked the guy if he'd had cancer yet, of course. I was just gobsmacked to realise that forty years after the advent of second-wave feminism, still the baby question came with the presumption that that was what you would, inevitably, be doing – you being a woman.

And as I got older, and it was clear I wasn't going along the baby route, it seemed not being a mother was as compelling a defining characteristic as actually being one – even though you didn't do anything to put yourself in that category. It felt transgressive to admit I didn't want to reproduce. 'Is there any woman in here tonight who has decided she doesn't want to have children?' I quizzed an audience one evening. I was compèring a show I produced for several years, called *Funny Girls*, featuring Irish comediennes. I'd been talking about this issue. One woman put up her hand. 'And when did you come to that realisation?' I asked her.

'After I had my fourth,' she said.

Howls of laughter from the mainly female house ensued, expressing, as her response had, the complexity of the baby issue, even when your answer is the apparently conventional 'Yes, please, I'll have some.'

Sometimes, given the preponderance of the notion 'women: have kids, sure what else would you be doing?',

I'd wonder was I the only one who had read that glut of books about the reality of children. The ones with outraged titles, like *Why Did Nobody Tell Me?*, *I Hate Being Mommy* and *Ah, For God's Sake, This Hurts*. Was I the only one who had had this sort of birthing conversation with a girlfriend?

'So, on a scale of one to ten, how painful was it *really?*'

'A hundred.'

Was I the only one who looked at drowning polar bears on telly and thought, There's probably enough of us humans on the planet already, and my instinctive desire not to have children is a tuning-in to the requirements of Mother Nature?

Another quirk about getting on with being childless was the pressure I felt whenever mums I knew asked what I was up to. I felt they expected a fabulous extended monologue of 'Oh. Wow. Where to begin! Just done dotting the final Is and crossing the last Ts on my latest novel! The fifteenth or eighteenth, whatever, can you believe? And I've just been commissioned to do a new series for RTÉ, under their strict usual artistic guideline that it cost nothing! So I'm putting a hidden camera in my hairline whenever I go out (which I'm always doing), and filming anything interesting that happens to me (which is everything, mostly)! Oh, and my MA! What can I say? Who could have guessed a thesis on "The Role of the Heart-warming Chat in Late-twentieth-century Irish-lady-writing" could just go on and on and on like it has? My MPhil last year, on "Comparative Windbags in Contemporary Irish Media", was a doddle compared.

Plus I'll be climbing Machu Picchu for the deaf/blind, at some stage, later in the week ...'

I'd find myself feeling guilty that generally I had nothing more exciting to say in answer to 'What are you doing?' than 'Oh. You know. Just had breakfast and sort of thinking about a cup of tea in the near future, with perhaps a biscuit or some cheese. Plus I'll be putting the bins out, at some stage, later in the month ...' There was guilt that the womb energy not expended on progeny didn't miraculously shift to other areas of life and turn me into Super-duper-high-achiever No-kids Lady. I was still the same doodler I was, before I became the Woman Who Doesn't Have Kids.

Then I'd think, Maybe if I'd had kids I'd have been more successful – the thought process of which went: Oh, sure, now I'm up at five a.m. with Billy, Milly, Lily and Fantine I might as well start a surprisingly well-organised and successful business. Not forgetting my daily hours of callisthenics and Pilates to maintain my ripped yummy-mummy tum between nappy changes. I'd look at busy mums I knew and couldn't help thinking I *should* be achieving more, seeing as I had roughly a thousand times more time than they had. Cancer at least let me off the hook in that guilt department.

I'd been experiencing a constant sense of guilt about not having kids. Now, after the blubber in Boots, I just felt sad about it. I thought about the lights of my life, my little niece and nephew. 'Look at all the pretty flowers in the park, all the different types and colours. Aren't they lovely?' the mother of one of her friends asked my beautiful blonde niece when she was three and a half years old.

'I didn't come here to look at flowers. I came here to play,' she replied.

'Does God make money?' wondered my then five-year-old handsome blue-eyed nephew to his dad.

To witness the blooming of those personalities, those unique intelligences coming into play with the world, exciting it with their originality – what a privilege. Imagine having brought them into the world. To have carried them within you. To have borne, suckled, nurtured and watched grow life that was of you, and ongoing beyond you. To be engaged in that most organic, most natural and biologically righteous cycle. These were now experiences beyond the biology that was me. Although once, cuddling my recently born nephew, he started doing that thing babies do with their lips to indicate a feed is due – those little smacking pouts. I was half tempted to put him to my breast, just to see what it felt like. I didn't, for fear my sister-in-law would see and be horrified. Later, when I told her about the urge I'd had, she laughed and said it was just as well I hadn't given it a whirl: he would have latched on extra hard if no milk was forthcoming, and the sum total of my experience would have been pain. Yet, particularly because I was about to lose one breast because of cancer, it seemed sad that my 'coat-hanger' nipples, which had 'nature's suckling device' written all over them, would never be engaged in such a core mammalian experience.

Could any expression of creativity be greater, any achievement feel more of an achievement than fine children? I asked myself, observing those two beloved and related little people, my niece and nephew, Rosa and Alexander.

Then again, you could give birth to hateful little shits, who milk the life out of you from day one, then end up on junk, in jail, track-marked and inked from forehead to shin, despite your heart-load of love, not to mention all the violin lessons, ballet and lacrosse; shits who darken your every day, blackening your name by an association you cannot sever. It's the last thing you think before you pop your clogs: was it worth the episiotomy scars? And the answer has to be a resounding, heart-rattling 'No', as you draw the last unhappy breath of your utterly ruined life. There was always that kind of comforting thought, the 'could be disastrous disappointment' perspective. Even if it was all now a moot point, the baby game was out for me.

I bought my sanitary things, and went back to the Metropole Hotel to lie on the bed and watch the ceiling some more before I performed a ludicrous gig with my girls – the show must go on.

7. Life Happens

I met a woman with a similar breast cancer to me but she had more comprehensive mortgage insurance than I, so her diagnosis meant her mortgage was paid. Now that's what I call winning the cancer lotto. Who knew you could get such cover? Who ever thought in a million years they'd get the Big C? Not me! HA! If I'd any inkling how common this cancer is, I would have had the same cover – horses bolting and stable doors slamming too late. There was no point in regrets. So the old maw of the mortgage still needed feeding, plus I was self-employed so there was no 'sick pay'. Pulling a chemo sickie wasn't an option then, but my lucky stroke was that I had work I didn't consider work – 'work' in the forty hours a week sense that you resent having to do it, but feck it, you have to live. As a supposedly grown-up forty-something, I was doing exactly the kind of thing I'd dreamed of as a child.

How did I come to be in a position in life where I achieved the livelihood I'd dreamed of, but thought impossible when I was young? Not through following a well-thought-out plan of action, that's for sure: I was all over the place for seven years after college. Half the time, I was thinking, When is proper life going to start? The other half I was trying to kick-start it. Only looking back, particularly through the goggles of breast cancer, did I realise there is no 'proper' when it comes to life. It's all just life. And this was mine.

I moved to London in the autumn of 1987. Far from greasepaint and the smell of the crowd, I ended up being an administrative temp with British Gas in Pimlico, a job that allowed me discover new depths of my inability to be organised, and develop such skills as 'how to look like you're inputting shit into a computer, while actually, literally, being asleep'. I'd buy the *Guardian* newspaper every Monday and read through the media-jobs section on the tube, desperate for something to pop out as 'me'. 'Media jobs' were what I had allegedly qualified to apply for. What would the ideal ad have said? 'Wanted, 21-year-old, farm-raised Irish girl, 5′ 9″, thin, brunette, bespectacled, with vague but jokey understanding of media, communications and the Odessa steps scene from *Battleship Potemkin*. Sincere, hardworking, clueless, unsure. Insecurity, lack of confidence, and inability to sustain being serious a plus – excellent pay, lovely conditions and an assurance of making it in a fluffy delicious delightful hilarious manner in showbiz. Only Pisceans with initials AG and an aversion to jellied eels need apply.'

Though I applied and interviewed for a few jobs,

I never did come across the kind of thing that had me thinking, Yes! I'd scan the ads, be repelled by the options, then feel like vomiting with anxiety about 'what happens next', life-wise. Most lunchtimes I'd run round the corner from the British Gas offices to the nearby Tate Gallery, the original one, which is now Tate Britain. The grand sweep of its entrance steps and regal breadth of the Thames were eyefuls of quick freedom. Inside, to spend thirty minutes in the space and light afforded to revered art was a heartening contrast to the banality of stuffing envelopes with final notices, or cat-napping over a dusty file drawer, in a stale office for hours. I. WANTED. THE. LIFE. OF. AN. ARTIST. How? I'd have little weeps there, under a famous painting, or beside a chunk of priceless sculpture, then dash back to work. I felt lost.

During my British Gas months there was an unexpected hurricane, an unbelievable inferno in King's Cross underground station, the shocking quashing of the Birmingham Six's first full appeal, while inside the fluorescent-lit open-plan office, the paperwork of the gas business trundled on. Regardless, I longed for anything other than squeezing onto the rush-hour tubes and buses I got to and from work each day, in between the time entirely wasted except that I was pulling in a wage. On the day of a long-time employee's retirement, fake flowers would be festooned around their desk in celebration, like the grave of someone newly dead. Why not have a papier-mâché headstone propped in their seat too, I'd think. It was all so morose. Retirees' family members would come in at the end of the day. I'd watch the cava and finger food send-offs through the glass wall of the manager's office – 'I raise this plastic container of economical bubbles to your lifetime's work. Here, have a sausage roll. And a Tunnock's tea cake. Now goodbye for ever.' Oh, God, what a piece of work is a man, how noble in reason, how infinite in faculty, how commonly capable of spending a lifetime pushing bulk-printed paper. 'What is this quintessence of dust?' was the opinion I evolved of each disconnection notice I stuffed into an envelope. Note to any south-east UK OAPs who received such in the winter of 1987–8: nobody told me the aged were exempted from disconnection in the cold months. Sorry.

I left that job come spring. Through participating in various drama and improvisation workshops, I got involved with a theatre-in-education company, devising and performing a show about apartheid. We toured England and Scotland at a time when events were escalating towards Nelson Mandela's release and the end of apartheid. After the show ended, I went to Moscow with a London-based youth-theatre company, at a time when events were escalating towards the end of Communism. Then, back in London, I ended up signing on at the social-welfare office at a time when circumstances were escalating towards me being penniless. Over the next few years I went on to create and produce performance-art pieces, performance poetry, and give multiple performances of 'Yeah, I am looking for a proper job' to my dole officer. There was the children's show, *The Bunyip and the Black Billabong*, I created with an Australian friend. I was the Bunyip, a sort of Aussie outback Abominable Snowman. The costume was a full, heavy, manky furry monstrosity, borrowed from a cheapo panto company. Somebody's cat had once pissed on it. The whiff of moggy wee, heat-softening latex and my sweat added nausea to the smorgasbord of delights experienced in taking that show round East End playgroups throughout a stupidly hot London summer.

Then there was the cabaret, songs by a fuddy-duddy Oxbridge twenty-something, all in ye olde Flanders and Swann mould – 'Lovely man, Jesus, up on the cross [something something], God what a loss', a sample lyric – a highlight of which was performing that song for OAPs in a Jewish community centre in Golders Green, fuddy-duddy pounding out his tunes on a clanging upright, us all forgetting the half-learned lyrics at a crucial moment during the dramatic cruciform-effect in the choreography.

Among the 'us' were two girls with whom I formed a trio, Doris Karloff, and for two erratic years, 1989 and 1990, we followed a strict artistic manifesto: 'Let's do anything that comes into our heads.' If you ever saw three people riding the London tube together, one in pyjamas, overcoat, outsize shoes and fake facial hair, one in a plastic mac over underwear, one in black with a bald pate, white makeup and massive black plastic gloves (I was trying to channel Max Wall), that was us. Why were we doing it? Why not? Then, at Covent Garden, we bumped into an old college friend of mine, already laying the foundations of her career as a serious TV journalist, and she went, 'Anne? Is that you?' just as I'd clocked and was trying to ignore her. That was the last time I went out and about sporting the bald-pate look until I got cancer.

'Hi,' I said, trying to sound as normal as one can, dressed like an idiot for no apparent reason in broad daylight in a foreign capital.

'Anne, what are you doing?' she asked.

If you were ever walking up Carnaby Street in 1989 and saw a bunch of rubbish bags suddenly stand up and walk around on gold boots while squirting a trail of tomato sauce, that was us. Our motivation? We'd been commissioned to create some 'street theatre'. Strictly speaking what we 'devised' wasn't within that remit, but we were being true to our 'whatever comes into our heads' guiding principle. If you were in a London cabaret club *circa* 1990 and saw three women doing sketches like a mock shampoo ad, 'Solve your probs *pour le* hair': us. Or if you were at a green-issues convention and saw a rather odd 'Is it funny or what?' sketch-and-song show called *When Did You Last Kill a Chicken?*: us. Or you spotted a street version of *Batman and Robin* on the West Piazza in Covent Garden, and you couldn't quite figure what was going on: us again.

In between such shenanigans, I survived variously by signing on and/or doing bitty jobs: cleaning at building sites all over London; catwalk modelling at hair shows; bar work on a boat moored at Embankment; cigarette promotions in suburban corner shops; assistant in the Science Museum; a telephone surveyor; an office temp, who, when the job involved typing, would arrive with pockets full of Tipp-Ex paper. My typing always had a distinctive stucco vibe to it, which was nice when employers prized a certain tactile quality to their correspondence. Not that I ever met one who did.

My default casual job was 'wenching'. When I first read the ad for a 'Wench in Medieval Restaurant', in the back of the *Stage* newspaper, I thought of lovingly re-enacted ye olde dining experiences, roast geese, the music of lutes, and wearing of fab corsetry (for some reason). Wrong! Located in old ivory-storage cellars near Tower Bridge, I suppose the dining area did have a medieval vibe, but more in the sense of 'dungeon' than 'banqueting hall'. The floor was stone flags, the walls and low-arched ceilings exposed brick, and there was an underlying dankness, perhaps because, as well as being underground, it was near the Thames. The trapped tourists were squashed together at long tables in narrow alcoves that ran perpendicular to the main concourse. That concourse was the 'stage'.

The medieval performers were a hotch-potch of out-of-work actors, balladeers, stage-fighters, a strong man of indeterminate age – you wouldn't have been surprised if he'd said 'Working the Victorian freak tents was my favourite gig' – a magician of indeterminate nationality, who dressed as if he'd strayed in from *Ali Baba*, the Christmas panto. There was an ageing tubby drag queen, an obese chap with bad feet, who was King Henry VIII, a rough and ready singer, who played Anne Boleyn but changed into an East End floozy by the night's end and rounded off the proceedings by barking out 'My Old Man Said Follow the Van' while she pranced up and down the stone corridor of a stage in a tired approximation of 'bawdy hoofing'.

The wench job entailed polishing all the cutlery, laying place settings, then dressing up in cheap-cotton maxis and mop caps, to sing while the punters entered, then serve their food, keep their jugs of manky wine and beer filled, be medieval / *Carry On* cheeky with them (my own addition to the job spec, to amuse myself), dance and sing along to the medieval (not) ballad accompaniment, such as the medieval (not) classic 'The Leaving of Liverpool'. I worked from six p.m. to eleven, for eleven pounds a night cash in hand when I started in 1988.

You had to laugh. And I tried to. The thing I'm most thankful to that place for, apart from all the handy 'scrape the bottom of the barrel' work when I was broke, is that it was where I met a couple of my ever-after soul-mate London girlfriends.

The wenches were a mix of girls starting out in dancing / acting / performing, actresses at mid-point career slumps, or performers at the end of careers like professional ice-skating or dance. Or, an anomaly, Spaniards because the manager was Iberian. A post-peak chorus dancer mentioned one night that she was considering working in a hostess bar because it paid exponentially better than our medieval pay rates. All you had to do, she said, was wait at the bar in the club. Men came in, and if they picked you, you sat with them, chatted, got them to buy champagne, 'drank' with them (you chucked yours on the floor when they weren't looking), then got them to buy more. Your 'pay' was commission on champers sold. It sounded like a dirty, sleazy, underworld kind of job – so naturally I thought I'd give it a whirl.

Through a Soho man I knew, let's just call him Mr Devil, I sourced such a club in Mayfair. When I buzzed the bell, a tall, slender, well-groomed lady answered. I expressed my interest in working there and she showed me in. I was rather disconcerted to see women, like me, mid-twenties, standing around in their underwear – not big knickers and modest brassière underwear either. No, the kind of undies that the word 'smalls' was invented for, thong-territory smalls that made a svelte young woman's body look somehow more naked, not less. Maybe the madam saw the startled look in my eyes. Had I not realised, she asked, that to be a hostess in her club you had to wear just lingerie? No, evidently I had not, and there was no way I was going to sit near nudie with some suits just because they were paying. For starters, my stomach wasn't toned (joke). It was an insight into the world of macho corporate bonding if, yuck, nothing else. But the funny thing I recall about that story is, I know the madam meant to say 'lingerie' but – and maybe this was just her slight Caribbean accent – what she actually said was 'You know you have to wear laundry here?' As I trundled away into the Mayfair night, I choked laughing at the idea of a job hanging out with business prats, draped in dirty socks and bedclothes for their sleazy delectation.

Such were the lower ends of the dead ends one might wind up in, while trying to be a 'something' with nothing to back the Dream. The seediest job I actually did was writing sex telephone messages for the business of my acquaintance Mr Devil. For a minimal fee, I wrote and recorded detailed erotic scenarios. I put so much work into those scripts, figuring if I were calling a phone-sex line, the feasibility of the sexual happening would matter to me, the sense of 'Wow, I can see this situation actually occurring.' And that would ratchet up the erotic intensity, and the guys would get value for their masturbatory telephone spend. The authorities had brought in new rules about the amount of *ad hoc* vocalisation allowed, Mr Devil said. Previously he'd run lines with no worked-out script, just women moaning a lot, and sucking oranges to give a sloppy wet sound, while going, 'Oh, just imagine what I'm doing' occasionally. You could no longer pay premium rates to hear someone moaning in a manner that might indicate 'erotic shenanigans' as much as 'sloppy eater'. It amuses me when I think back, my concern with narrative feasibility, which was hardly a priority for a chap in the phone-sex scenario, receiver in one hand, the other doing something you'd really rather not think about.

'Occupation?' the nurse asked. Shit, I thought. Why do they always have to ask such tough questions? It was 1991 and I was registering with my local family planning clinic in south London. I never knew quite how to articulate officially what it was I did. 'I'm a performer,' I answered.

Her pen paused above the form she was filling out. Her expression suggested that she did not recognise that noun as an occupation, and also that she suspected I was joking. The word echoed in the ensuing silence between us. 'I'm a performer,' I had said. In a family planning clinic? Wasn't that like saying 'I'm a goer'? 'I do be at it'? That I took the procurement of birth control as seriously as a bonky British comedy – *Carry On Up My Uterus!* – because, being Irish, I was so innately hung up about sex that I couldn't enter into the dynamics of being fitted for a contraceptive cap without reducing the interaction to a skit? 'Erm, comedian,' I corrected myself. 'I mean comedian.' Like that was any better.

That word didn't rest any more comfortably with me, even though that was what I was doing, or trying to do at the time. I'd left my Doris Karloff girls and had started doing solo stand-up. My motivation was one-fold: to earn some money. There was a big and burgeoning club comedy scene in London, and if you could establish yourself, there was the potential for regular paid gigs. It didn't seem a huge leap from all I'd done up to then to be able to write gags and develop a standard twenty-minute set to work around the circuit. It couldn't be that tough, could it?

I booked a load of 'open spots', unpaid five-minute try-outs in comedy clubs, then sat down to write the hilarious material that would earn me a living and bankroll my ongoing more important quest: to find the performance form I really wanted to work in. Facing the naked page, I was bludgeoned by the reality: what the fuck am I going to talk about onstage? Stuff loosely based on my experience? Sex telephone lines: *Why don't they have specialist services, like one for fans of bestiality? Phone up and you just hear, 'Baa, baa.' Or one for masochists? Phone up and you hear, 'Hi, thank you for calling, please hold the line. This call is costing you ten pounds seventy-five a minute.* Or beliefs: *I'm a feminist. Like, I was in a queue the other day. There's was a numbered ticketing system. I took a ticket. I'm waiting there. And the man behind the counter says, 'You, that girl there, you're next.' I said, 'Excuse me, did you call me a girl? I'm not a girl, I'm a number, OK?' Or cliché: We were poor growing up, but my mum was brilliant with poverty. She'd say to us, just remember – the best things in life are free. Which was our cue to go out shoplifting. We were so poor we'd come home and find that we'd only stolen stuff that'd been on special offer.*

And ba-dum-ching – not! Club comedy, I soon discovered, wasn't really my bag. Not only did I struggle to write really good material but it was a struggle to find a definitive, sure-fire comedy voice and get a sense of where I might fit into the London comedy scheme of things. 'It takes seven years to become a comic,' some comic mused to me. I didn't have seven years, I just wanted to earn some cash onstage pronto, with stuff I'd written, rather than serve sub-edible food to tourists in Tower Hill, or wash new-build office interiors with buckets of freezing water in the City or, worst case, find myself thinking, What the hey? I can throw away champagne, in my knickers, with wankers – at least it pays.

Trouble was, I had this niggling old feeling of being the outsider, of being, somehow, too totally different. Actually, I *was* different from the vast majority of the other comics in that I had boobs and no penis. Most were men, and I came to see it as a man's kind of gig. The scene was very 'ladsy', robust, rippling with machismo and testosterone-tinged competitiveness. I felt like a delicate little comedy ovary, twittering my novice little Fallopian gags, outside the overpowering scrotum of ballsy big hairy-arse real-man comedy. 'Wank,' some folk might say, but that did rather seem like the basic cock-and-cunt of it to me. I was fucked, basically. Oops – sorry for that burst of fuckety-do-dah language. I just got caught in a jizz-spunk blur of remembering those knob-packed clubs.

But I could be a motherfucking tough poonani when I needed to be so, head down, I got stuck in, and sucked it up for a couple of years. And, in that time hacking around, I started to get paid sets in smaller clubs. I was OK. But who wants to be just 'OK'? I wanted to be brilliant or *nada*. 'She was all right, I'd fuck her,' I recall the compère of an infamously rowdy south London club say, as I was leaving the stage after doing a spot one night – it was a typical 'fun' comment of that ex-con 'comedy character' to a new lady performer. But I hated hearing it in reference to myself. It was all so ugly. I just kept ploughing on because this was how to learn the comedy skill, wasn't it? They say you need to develop a skin as thick as an elephant's to be a stand-up, so wasn't I gonna darn well stick it till I was thoroughly thick, grey, wrinkly and tough as Dumbo all over? I wasn't so sure.

I applied for and won a scholarship to do a postgraduate acting course at The Academy of Live and Recorded Arts, a drama school with beautiful studios and grounds located in a Victorian former orphanage in Wandsworth, south London. The training was excellent and comprehensive: radio and camera acting, style in theatre, movement, dance, vocal training, stage fight, singing, auditioning, sight-reading, approach to Shakespeare, mime, how to talk posh and feel relaxed with people who had posh accents, native or no, addressing you as '*daaaahling*', not an official module, just something that happened and was apparently necessary in the field. The year there was thoroughly wonderful, like being in the Fame Academy of *Fame*. I may even have worn leg warmers with my leotard and jazz shoes in movement class …

I auditioned for lots after I graduated, until there was a cattle call for the chorus of the long-running musical *Les Misérables*, then playing at the Palace Theatre in London's West End. I got a time slot at the stage door, and had a couple of hours to kill. That day I was utterly broke. Literally, I had no money. Not even the change to get a coffee. I walked through Soho, scanning the pavement for coins, thinking, This is like a scene in a film where the magic turnaround thing happens. Mr The One finally appears, and whisks me away to have one of the finest lattes known to man, then offers me a starring role in a major Thing, his hand in marriage, a cream bun and a second finest latte. In one fell swoop life, somehow, turns around, dismal becomes fabadoobie, loneliness flips into love and being lost becomes being found by those Super Trouper lights.

In lieu of none of that happening, I went to Burger King at Piccadilly Circus and sat in a toilet cubicle (free) in the disinfectant pong of all fast-food bogs until it was time to sing. Eight shows a week in a chorus, I thought. And I'm twenty-seven years old. Broke. My home is a squat. The last man I was involved with was so permanently buzzed on coke it was like dating the Duracell bunny. My only regular work is as a serf. I live on lentil soup and oatcakes. I've almost considered being naked for a living. I don't want to be a luvvie. *Macbeth, Macbeth, Macbeth*: I loathe stupid theatrical superstitions. And I don't want to make my peers those geezers playing London comedy clubs either. And everything I've done for the last six years isn't really what I wanted. And through it all I've been fighting the loneliness of fear, feeling lost for having no roots, and missing the closeness of someone to love. All of which, I'd actually think, will end up in cancer. Though ostensibly I'd developed a neck like a jockey's bollocks, inside I felt childish and frightened, and how much can your shaky inner girlie spirit take? When I got back to the theatre to audition I met a girl coming out whom I'd met earlier in the cattle queue. 'I don't think either of us is right for this. Look at the promo photos. They need girls with bigger tits for the costumes,' she said. By then I couldn't have given a hoot if my hooters weren't up to the job. I had decided I was moving back to Dublin even before I auditioned and didn't get a call back.

Back in Dublin I started gigging in my brother's club, the Comedy Cellar. The atmosphere was very supportive after the anonymity of the London scene. Small and cosy suited me. And I had the massive love and support of my good brother Kevin. I began to revel in writing ridiculously Irishy material, peppered with Gaelic words, and with the cadence and references of what, I finally understood, was really, truly home. It was a combination of that connection to a creative source and, for the first time, really sensing and appreciating the meaning of 'roots', of feeling safe, and then of fortuitously meeting some comediennes with whom I had total comedy empathy that led to what felt like the break I'd always longed for: The Nualas. The 'job' that helped keep me going financially, but didn't feel like 'work' when I was going through chemo.

8. A/C

What does 'having chemotherapy' actually entail? One guy I met said he was expecting 'a satellite-dish yoke' or 'a gun thing'. Confusing cancer treatment with sci-fi movies? Easy enough: I'd an image of tubes and pipes, of personnel in white coats one side of a reinforced-glass observation window, you on the other, in the white-tile isolation chamber, strapped to a thing while another thing pumps the what-have-you into your whatever, and after that your life turns into something from another type of movie – an extended sick-bed scene from an eighties AIDS drama. But you live, just about. And repeat.

Then suddenly you're there. You're finding out. It's you having chemo, because you have cancer, and you still can't quite believe it. On 20 July 2011, thirteen days after the first mention of the C-word, we, my sister and I, were back in the waiting area of the hospital oncology unit – a section of corridor with cramped plastic seating.

What do I recall? That it was crowded, the air stagnant with everyone's breath and body heat. There was a grey pallor on some patients' faces but none looked absolutely emaciated. There was a low-level frisson of energy, tension, apprehension in 'the area', compounded by the inescapable large flat-screen television, playing *The Jeremy Kyle Show*. Which struck me as a peculiar choice of waiting room 'entertainment': 'We're not talking about your son! We're talking about WHY YOU ARE SUCH A BAD MOTHER!' His horribly aggressive banter was hardly a distracting salve for people here, of all places.

A door opened and a nurse with a clipboard called my name. Una and I followed her through to the other side. My first impression was of the calm of the place, especially compared to where we'd just been: there were six powder blue La-Z-Boy recliner leather armchairs, three facing three. Four were occupied by relaxed female patients. Bright summer light streamed in from the wall of windows at one end. It could almost have been a beautician's, except for the intravenous tubes running into an extended arm of each seated woman, wearing either a wig or a turban that suggested she was bald beneath. And the busy nurses to-ing and fro-ing, attending to these seated people, and other patients unseen, either side of the partition walls; the concentrated activity and pervading atmosphere that all added up to 'Hospital' or, more specifically, 'Oncology Day Ward'.

My sister and I stood in the wide aisle between the seats, taking it in. I was trembling. I knew Una was upset. How had life suddenly landed us here? We'd been planning a long break in Greece, Una's first country of residence after college, home of some of her longest-standing friends and a favourite place in the world for both of us. We hadn't been there in yonks. Now, this place was the only out-of-the-ordinary one we'd be visiting all summer. 'It felt like life went off on a parallel track that day we were told. Afterwards I was looking at people on the street feeling like I was in a separate world, thinking constantly, My sister has cancer,' she told me. I would have felt the same, had it been her. More so: I'm more extreme. I would have found unbearable the pressure of not knowing would she be all right in the end. I felt bad that this had been put upon her. I'm the elder, by thirteen months, the big sister, usually the one to be needed, not needy.

We were still in shock, standing there.

'Choose a chair,' a nurse zipping by told us. Left, right, which one? The two middles were free. I took the right-hand one. Did it matter? I wanted my hand held, wanted the nurse to point out where I should put my bum, it being the first time, feeling sick to the stomach with it all, feeling, too, like a child again, being told what to do, wanting to be told what to do, feeling odd, lost, nervous. The strangeness of sitting into that soft seat, an ordinary armchair elevated to the realm of medical drama. There was a hospital table on wheels one side, intravenous stand and drip monitor the other, square of rail overhead, with attached curtain, if you needed to be screened off.

'You want trumpets or something, some ceremony,' Una noted wryly. Something to mark the beginning of this enormous thing for you. YOU are about to begin

CHEMOTHERAPY! Almost ridiculous that YOU are starting the thing that belonged to other people's stories. CHEMO! For God's sake! Stupid, unbelievable, so incredible it made you want to weep: it was you beginning that mythic medical process. And, also, it was just another day in a busy hospital oncology ward. If not trumpets, could there be access to some sacrament perhaps, something to honour, augur, mark what was to come, what was about to commence? The sense that major life events require a ceremony of acknowledgement was ingrained in me by Catholicism, I guess. The point was: this was a major life event.

A nurse plonked a tray containing two bags of clear liquid and a packaged cannula on the table and went off again. Underneath was my hospital file. I began to flick through it. I was looking for the MRI report, the one that said something about the 'multiple tiny lesions scattered throughout the left breast' that the surgeon had mentioned; the diagnosed reason a mastectomy was unavoidable. I wanted to see it written down and here was the opportunity. I wanted to read the whole thing, all the detail, as if it might contain something I hadn't been told, something I ought to know, something that said everything of all that I was going through. I somehow suspected that the worst was being withheld. Why wouldn't I, given the historic medical culture of the country I was in? The well-documented regressive, religion-driven medical regime wherein consultants were gods, doctors deities, and nurses their hardened handmaidens, all together in their general dispensation of 'care', dismissing patients as too plebeian to understand the whats and whys of processes being exercised on their bodies. The subjection of women to unnecessary hysterectomies and, worse, the Catholic-doctrine-encouraged mutilation of symphysiotomy in childbirth when the practice was regarded as barbaric in other developed jurisdictions – oh, ranty ranty rant. If you were to put being a woman in an Irish hospital in an historical context there was a fierce number of reasons to get your shackles in a twist. I wanted to know the exact whys and wherefores of everything being done unto my body because it was the only one I had, however common bodies are in the hospital setting! I hated that I felt as if I was 'snooping' through my hospital records. Why shouldn't I be allowed read the records 'officially' articulated on my behalf. A passing nurse saw me and Una with our noses in my chart. 'Sorry, you can't read that,' she said, taking the file from us. 'You might misinterpret it.' I was, to put it mildly, miffed.

My three distractions in that whole initial period of diagnosis and chemotherapy were information, information, information: I just read and read and read everything I could till my mind was a swamp of cancer terminology: lymphovascular invasion, cytokines, histopathology, angiogenesis, neoplasm, carcinoma, sarcoma, metastasis, rads, nodes, nips, suspicious lump, tits, death. I slopped around the Internet sucking it all up, filling the time between the actual stuff of treatments.

Like now, the needle of the cannula being inserted; I asked the nurse to use a vein in the back of my hand. She said the crook of the arm was less painful. But not for me.

Can you generalise about such things?

Part of the experience is: you get used to being pricked by needles. Each session requires needle-aspirated blood sampling beforehand, for blood count tests to make sure your immune system is up to the onslaught of poison. If the oncologist isn't happy with the results, chemotherapy will be delayed. First time round, my bloods had been taken five days previously, when I'd had the introductory meeting with the oncologist.

'Just a small scratch,' the nurse said, me holding my hand in a fist to get the vein up. I'd get used to that expression: it's what they all said, inserting the needle. Every time I'd think, This isn't actually what I'd call a 'scratch'. A scratch is, say, a cat accidentally tickling its claw along your skin. This feels more like something that should be termed 'a wee stab in the hand' or, more poetically, 'a small OH FUCK'. The cannula needle delivers the thin plastic tube into your vein; it is attached to the exterior plastic taps through which treatment will be delivered. The tap part is taped securely across your skin once the tube has been snugly needled in. Objectively: the insertion hurts a little, sometimes more than others – depending on the technique and skill of the oncology nurse, and, I came to realise, on the physical form of the body. Some days my body felt more sensitive than it did on others, and certainly as treatment proceeded I was more tender, pain-sensitive and downright poison-aching all over. I explained as much to my local friendly pharmacist, Michael, and he gave me a tube of Emla, local anaesthetic cream for rubbing on injection sites before needles. I also started bringing painkillers to the hospital and popping them when it was coming up to needle-procedure time. Whether either of these things was 'allowed' I didn't enquire: dealing with my own low pain-threshold was the more pertinent concern.

First off, that day, my cannula tap was hooked up to a large bag of saline solution and a smaller one of liquid steroids. The saline was to flush the veins open and hydrate; the steroids to aid the body to tolerate the sudden influx of poison. They felt cool, draining into the vein, the cannula constantly slightly painful in the back of my hand. My sister was by my side on a small uncomfortable stool – she'd had to go a-huntin' to find that bum-ache to sit on: extra seats were in short supply on the oncology day ward. From what I gathered, the hospital didn't want to encourage day patients turning up with an entourage of support. Nowhere-to-sit was one discouragement. Another was the notice informing patients they were allowed only one 'visitor'. Some ignored these signals and instructions, or maybe just didn't notice them, in this weird situation at this weird time of all our lives.

The intravenous saline and steroids took about an hour. Then the nurse came back wearing a white plastic apron and latex gloves, looking like a kinky cook, delivering my noxious lunch, which she was carrying on another plastic tray: four large plastic syringes, two of clear liquid, two of lurid red – the adriamycin cyclophosphamide, the A/C chemotherapy. Then she got another nurse and together they cross-checked, aloud, to each other my file prescription, the syringe contents, the details on my paper hospital bracelet. They asked me my name, my date of birth. In a way this rigmarole felt like the ceremony Una had said she longed for. It was a precaution: the syringes contained poison, modulated to the threshold that my health and body mass could withstand. One misadministration and there'd be trouble – I'd heard an apocryphal story of a patient, in A.N. Other country, dying rather hurriedly after being administered someone else's chemotherapy. The formality of the cross-check before delivery honoured the gravity of what was about to happen, a life marker for me and my sister – both of us still in disbelief that any of it was happening.

A/C is administered by hand. Each syringe is, in turn, attached to one of the little taps of the cannula protruding from the vein and the contents slowly injected into the body. The nurse sat opposite me; the hand being injected rested on a pillow on the hospital table that had been positioned between us. It was done this way, rather than through a drip, because the nurse has constantly to monitor that the contents of the syringe don't leak outside the vein as they are being pumped into the bloodstream. 'If they did it would burn the surrounding cells, and you'd need a skin graft,' the nurse explained, when I asked. Lovely. So can you imagine what it might be doing to your insides? I could, right then. Two words: Hieronymus Bosch.

She did the bright red ones first – 'Red Devil', as it's known in Internet chat rooms.

A book I'd been given suggested you visualise your chemotherapy as 'a clear, sparkling, health-giving fluid'. Further on it said, 'Chemotherapy was developed from mustard gas.' I never got past thinking, Someone's pumping the equivalent of battery acid into me.

It was poignant, upsetting, the sight of it being injected in, the nurse slowly compressing the syringe, the noxiousness of the contents, the fact that in killing all fast-growing cells, not just the cancerous, it would thwack the hair, affect the skin, mouth, ovaries, womb and God knows what else. It's counter-intuitive that to get well you have to be made ill. That you had willingly to lay open your veins to *this*. And you never even *felt* unwell in the first place. Yet if you'd waited until you 'felt ill' it would have been too late for any of this life-saving treatment, therein some of the contradictions of cancer.

The back of my hand felt sore: the tug of the cannula in the vein, or the effect of the chemicals squeezing into it?

I chatted incessantly to the nurse, picking her brains about the process, her experience, aware she must have been asked and have answered these questions innumerable times, that this conversation was, for her, additional work. When will the side-effects kick in? What will they be like? Are they the same for everyone? Are they cumulative? Will it affect the veins in the back of my hand? It must be the short straw of an oncology shift, having to do the manually injected chemos. A different nurse administered it each of my four times.

The four chunky plastic canisters took just over an hour to empty. Afterwards I was told to check my temperature overnight: if it went over 38°C I was to call the hospital immediately, whatever the time, day or night. I'd need intravenous antibiotics immediately. And that was it. Una and I cycled back to my apartment. I felt very dizzy and tired, wobbly on my bike. Una dropped me off. A cousin who'd been through breast cancer chemo told me that after the first time, when she got home, she painted the bathroom: a combination of energy from steroids, desire to proceed as if everything was normal and being handy with a roller and emulsion. Me, I went to bed, lay wide awake and exhausted at the same time.

The steroids gave me insomnia, made me feel hyper and tense, made my jaws grind and my pupils dilate, as if I'd popped cheap speed. They're the crack cocaine of chemotherapy. Or, as my friend Michelle put it, 'You look like a crack addict in a hot-air balloon.' In addition to the intravenous bag at the hospital, I was prescribed them in tablet form for the following two days.

Other medications prescribed with the chemo included an oral fungicide, a drug to stave off stomach ulcers, painkillers, anti-emetics and a very expensive new hi-tech medication, Neulasta. It stimulates the manufacture of white blood cells in the bone marrow, boosting the immune system in the face of chemo-attack. Otherwise, the body couldn't tolerate the 'dense-dose' fortnightly schedule of chemotherapy, such as I was on. Neulasta comes in a syringe, ready for injecting. It has to be kept in the fridge for hi-tech freshness. I was prescribed one after each of my eight chemotherapy treatments, to be injected the day after treatment. A nurse came to my apartment the afternoon after the first chemo to show me how to do the injection. I practised on a little spongy plastic pillow a few times, then tried it myself in the stomach, a jab in the flab, which didn't hurt at all that first time. But by the fourth or fifth chemo, the injection became quite stingy. By then, after a couple of months of chemo, my body was constantly sore and sensitive all over.

The nurse gave me a disposal canister for used spikes, a bright yellow plastic box. I left it on my kitchen counter. It screamed, 'Danger, Emergency, Attention, Achtung – Cancer Thingies' at me every time I made a cup of tea.

There was a comedy festival that weekend. We had two gigs in a 700-seat marquee in the Iveagh Garden, in central Dublin, on Friday and Saturday night. Performing was no problem. It was a heartening distraction, and empowering in the face of all the disempowerment cancer seemed to involve. At least I could continue to earn a living – at least I didn't have to stop working, and have the realities of illness take over everything.

When you're on chemo you have to be careful about hygiene, not being around people with colds or infections, not hanging out in leper colonies, that kind of thing, because your immune system is weakened. I ate a burger from a festival catering van and lived; the gigs were doable and great. I was beginning to think this was how my particular metabolism would handle it: no hitches. But on the fifth day, Sunday, it hit.

What does chemo-sickness feel like? Deep-gut nausea laced with flu-ache, dried-out eyes, sore mouth, headachy irritation topped with a general inability to do stuff, like you've been punched all over by fists of weird illness. My brain felt like it had shrunk inside my skull and my consciousness had lodged itself several centimetres apart from where it usually was. It felt like my head was really taking the brunt, buzzing, full, wobbly, seasick. Walking up the street, I felt like I was going to keel over. The life seemed to have drained out of me, the shine gone from my hair, the light from my eyes, of which one was now bloodshot. This was it: the feeling of being sick to go with the fact of being sick. The feeling of life powering on without you – and suddenly I couldn't but notice lots of babies. There seemed to be babies everywhere, in cafés, in pushchairs being wheeled along pavements, in the doorways of houses I passed, the 'wah-wah' of a newborn being prepared for an outing. I'm relegated to Nature's sick bay, I remember thinking. Step aside. Even my teeth hurt.

I learned to handle it by going to ground for three to four days each time. It was the steroids kept me going for the first couple of days, but when nausea kicked in I went to bed and stayed there. Some cancer veterans say, 'Get up, get out.' Not me. Bed, oh, lovely bed. Pillows, crisp sheets, snuggly duvet, the fantastic new mattress I eventually got in honour of the illness: these were a few of my best-loved things.

It feels like a sin to admit it in this day and age of we-all-have-to-rush-about, it feels like admitting to a sordid affair, but I love bed deeply – an affair chemo allowed me indulge. I slept a lot and could, almost, not feel guilty about it.

9. Positivity

'You've got to stay positive and push through the fatigue,' said a businessman I knew, talking more to himself than to me. He had stage-four bowel cancer, was on continuing rounds of debilitating chemotherapy. Yet the alarm was set for five thirty every single morning and he obeyed it. His tenacity and attitude were impressive, and I felt guilty that, though I did keep working, I didn't have the same determination to be positive. At all. 'Your attitude really makes a difference. You absolutely must proactively focus on positive thinking,' I kept being told. The day I was having my wig fitted, that's what the ladies in the shop were anxious to point out, THE IMPORTANCE OF POSITIVITY! One related the story of a close relation who had beaten ovarian cancer, when the prognosis had been imminent death. She'd visualised the cancer gone, and off it had toddled, and she's still alive today, years later. The power of mental attitude, positive thinking, visualisation: I should remember it. My friend Sue, whose mother had passed away from ovarian cancer, listened in silence. Driving me back to my apartment, she told me that her mother had done everything she could to survive her cancer; her attitude couldn't have been more positive as she endured every available conventional medical and alternative treatment, and engaged in daily visualisations of the tumour shrinking into oblivion, yet still ... 'What those women were saying isn't true,' she said. 'You can't just think yourself better.'

But that idea is strongly out there, with its unhelpful flipside that perhaps your mental attitude caused the cancer in the first place. It's become even more firmly entrenched in popular culture through all those recent pseudo-scientific best-selling books that expound the Law of Attraction, the idea that your thoughts entirely instigate your reality: 'The most powerful law that governs our lives', according to the author of *The Secret* and *The Power*, the two top sellers of the genre in the last decade. Books that pontificate about the amazing life that is your birth right, if only you will let it happen, if only you will direct your mind in that direction. And, like, if you're not having fun, or you're out and out suffering, hey man, wake up! Stop attracting that shit into your life already! It's your thoughts control the whole shebang, wow-wee!

The author makes claims that wouldn't be out of place in a fairy tale yet, extraordinarily, she and other proponents of extreme positivity posit serious scientific principle behind their theories, based in quantum physics. They take the rarefied notion that the act of observation affects the behaviour of sub-atomic particles, and conclude, therefore, that our thoughts utterly control reality. You can morph the world into the shape of your thinking! No consideration of the fact that we're macroscopic entities dealing with macroscopic things that obey macroscopic laws, that you cannot make direct inferences from the quantum world to the macroscopic world. A physics professor I know chuckled at the absurdity of the idea: 'If quantum physics led to such a malleable world, don't you think Einstein would have done something about his hair?' he said.

To quote American oncologist Siddhartha Mukherjee, who won a Pulitzer Prize in 2011 for his history of cancer *The Emperor of All Maladies*: 'A positive mental attitude does not cure cancer – any more than a negative mental attitude causes cancer.' Of un-prognosticated positive outcomes, he notes: 'We know there are spontaneous remissions in cancer, it's very well documented. Many cancers are chronic remitting relapsing diseases – that's their very nature.'

There's fascinating reading on the Internet while you're on chemotherapy. Did you know some people train for marathons while undergoing it? Some keep working forty-hour weeks. Others hardly notice anything different about their lives – except they're going to hospital every two to three weeks to be poison-injected because there's an uncontrolled abnormal cell growth happening inside them that would turn them to worm-lunch if they weren't being pricked with poison ...

I'd lie there, my mind running about their running: what kind of marathons were those other women training for? The twenty-six-mile crawl on hands and knees? What kind of job could those forty-hours-a-week women have been doing? Exploring the optimal comfy position in bed? And how did women go through this with kiddies? How did they feel this bad yet keep up the wife/mother front?

No more comparing yourself to other people, I'd demand of me, because now I had the ultimate excuse – cancer! But it was hard not to. Take this, from the blog of an American TV journalist. Similar in age (compare), she also had stage-three triple negative breast cancer and proactively helped beat it, she indicated, by regular exercise and adherence to 'a very pure diet'. Plus (compare) she was a super-successful journo: the national security correspondent for Fox News (well, even the most positive cancer stories had a downside).

She had pre-surgery chemo – same as me. She exercised throughout – same as me, in my dreams. She said that doing Pilates made her core muscles so strong that when she had the surgery, the orderlies didn't even have to lift her from the gurney to the bed, she could darn well shift her own butt onto that mattress. Hey, I wanted to be like that too! 'When it came time for surgery, the orderlies didn't have to lift *me* from the gurney. I did a triple somersault back-flip onto the bed, ended in a straddle split and the whole place burst into wild applause.'

She also jogged, noting that General David Petraeus would 'write late at night to see how I was doing and challenge me to a run'. Some name-check, huh? Like me saying, 'Martin McGuinness would text at all hours, challenging me to a post-treatment egg-and-spoon race up the Falls Road – I never knew was it encouragement or a threat but it sure kept me on my chemo-jogging schedule.'

It fascinated me how some women, Americans in particular, knew the precise titles of their cancer. In Internet chat rooms, the tag-line of posts, the abbreviation of their diagnosis: Dx 2/8/2010 IDC, 2cm, Stage II, Grade 2, 2/19 nodes, ER+/PR+, HER2 or Dx 4/6/2009 IDC, 2cm, Stage II, Grade 2, 0/1 nodes, ER+/PR+, HER2 or Dx 9/9/2008 IDC, 4cm, Stage IIIa, Grade 3, 0/23 nodes, ER+, HER2. Generally Irish women wouldn't be given that level of information to name their cancer thus: you'd have to rustle it out for yourself – as I did through the hospital freedom-of-information office, eventually. But being *au fait* enough with it to reduce it to the letter and numerals tag-lines? That was impressive. Or a bit obsessive.

Or was it necessary in the States, with a medical system that involved working out what you could afford to pay for, what you needed to survive – if you could afford it? 'First thing you need to get after a breast cancer diagnosis is a folder. There's going to be a lot of paperwork,' a US breast cancer site advised. In Ireland, it was different. You could survive with just one piece of paperwork, your appointment card, if you so wished. I ended up with lots because I collected all the reports, but here's an example of the old-school patient approach to hospital treatment. 'What kind of chemotherapy are you on?' I asked an elderly lady sitting near me one day.

'Oh, I don't know!' she said. She called to the nurse, 'Nurse, what am I on?'

'Taxol,' the nurse said.

'Taxol,' the woman repeated to me – which seemed to make as much sense to her as if the nurse had said, 'Leo Red Dry Cow Injector.'

Another Internet revelation was the terminology people used, like 'survivorship', as in 'I'm two years into my survivorship.' Life completely defined by the cancer experience, the time ever after contextualised in terms of your tumour, I thought, the word niggling me. It was too melodramatic, I figured, and isn't there enough language extant without having to mash up new words? Survivorship! Where next with all that? RIP, she's a year into her deathdom.

And don't talk to me about the 'Pink Ribbon journey' aesthetic. Who decided there was something pink and ribbony about freaking cancer? Pink, that anodyne shade for little girlies. At six even my niece was going, 'I hate pink.' It was banished from the palette of her life to be replaced by feisty red. Pink Ribbon: cancer? Online, from the States, there's no end to the permutations of Pink Ribbon product: Pink Ribbon 'what cancer cannot take from you' ceramic mugs (two, generously sized); Pink Ribbon floral-themed luncheon napkins (pack of twenty); Pink Ribbon acrylic cup (with straw); Pink Ribbon cupcake picks (pack of thirty-six); Pink Ribbon golf bag (by Wilson); Pink Ribbon feather boa; Pink Ribbon pasta (fourteen-ounce bag); Pink Ribbon keg of Pilsner (eighty-eight pints of rosy-hued lager); Pink Ribbon sticky-note cube; Pink Ribbon muffin cups (pack of seventy-five) – and one of those isn't true: guess which.

Seriously, isn't that like having rheumatoid arthritis

table runners or Hodgkin's lymphoma pot-holders? The commodification of illness, the odd commodities, the leap away from the reality of what IT IS. One day I even came across a recipe for Pink Ribbon Risotto: imagine, Arborio rice the colour of wane blood, to evoke Breast Cancer, for lunch? Hello, weird alert!

What was effortlessly positive was to share experience with other women. I met two who had been prescribed the same schedule as me, four A/C followed by four Taxol. Neither chemo adversely affected one woman, who said she 'flew through it'. The other was hospitalised after every A/C treatment and reacted so badly to Taxol it had to be stopped after the first time 'or else we'll be amputating your feet', her oncologist told her. Interesting that the effects could vary so much.

One piece of information I found repeatedly delivered to my face, as something to be positive about: BREAST CANCER IS SO COMMON – as if a gangrenous, oozing medieval pandemic casualty was historically to be comforted with the words 'But the Black Death, it's everywhere! It's trending!' Oh, well, then, hey nonny no, I feel better about my plague now you've pointed out that it's not so much being sick as being as fashion forward.

'I think I know more women with breast cancer than without,' one person actually said to me. Whatever was intended by the comment, and one can't assume it was necessarily negative, the implication was that they were equating breast cancer with something of a similar ubiquity to the common cold. That certainly was the impression I was left with. It felt negative, horribly dismissive.

'And it's so treatable now,' another person noted. 'It's like having acute appendicitis.' Erm, no, it's not, was all I felt, deep in my gut. Ultimately such comments were saying that to make anything of your illness is to make too big a deal of it – so could you please pretend it's nothing?

In a similar vein, you'd get the stories: the sister-in-law, the neighbour, the eighty-year-old granny who'd had your thing and flown through it. Although it wasn't said in so many words, it was made to sound like those rellies and acquaintances didn't so much have cancer as some manner of dainty wart, and hadn't so much endured months of treatment as had a restorative dainty-wart-removing holiday. Shtick that was just shy of 'Best thing that ever happened to them!' Like there was nothing negative about it at all. In fact, all things considered, bloody lucky you.

It was one thing I never wanted to hear: people telling me about the cancers of other people they knew. I could barely get my head around my own. The complex feelings and physical realities of it were not ameliorated by dismissive anecdotes, and such generalities. Better be silent.

'Now, Anne, don't be feeling sorry for yourself,' an aunt calling from England said, when she heard of my diagnosis, giving voice to the programme in my own rural Irish Catholic DNA.

'Arra, I will not,' that inner guide reassured me. 'I will keep a constant mindfulness of the miseries of plague, war, famine and economic hostility under which the majority, the less fortunate of this planet, labour, while paying commensurate observance to the fact that the medical system within which I am ensconced is by comparison a fortunate luxury, and remaining perpetually mindful of three key things. One, it could always be worse. Two, things have been historically shite in Ireland for ever so whatever hits you now is infinitely less than then, which leads to three – you are very, very, very lucky, whatever.'

I questioned the head off the nurse who administered my second dose. She said, 'The first is the worst. Now you know what to expect. Just drink lots of water. You'll be grand.' I wasn't. Really, what she should have said was that it's impossible to predict, reactions vary hugely. Because when I got sicker quicker, and for longer, second time round, again I was thinking, What's wrong with me? Snap out of it.

My brother Kevin gave me a book called *Your Life in Your Hands*, by Professor Jane Plant. I speed-read it one chemo-flattened afternoon, utterly nauseous with a sensation that my digestive tract was rotting, and with how sloppily non-proactive I was by comparison with this feisty, intelligent, hectoring academic (compare). Given a few months to live because of recurrent breast cancer, she undertook extensive research that led her to this conclusion: no dairy ever again. She made a compelling case in the book, advising a diet that avoids all animal protein and is rich in fresh organic vegetables, fruits, nuts and berries – the kind of stuff we all know, yet somehow kebab houses continue to thrive.

I devoured the book, vowing to organise my diet according to her rules because it seemed remiss to be accepting thousands of euro worth of medical treatment, and not make whatever suggested effort I could in my non-hospital life. Then – I don't know what happened – cheese crept in, the idea of a ham sandwich beat the thought of tofu and broccoli delight, someone said, 'Will you take a biscuit?' and I said, 'Yes.' With the attendant guilt that a bourbon cream wasn't just useless calories any more: it was a potential killer.

The funny thing was, the person regularly offering the bourbon creams was the tea lady on the oncology day ward. The patients got endless offers of tea, sandwiches and biscuits while they were being treated. I loved the oddness of intravenous poison going into the back of one hand, while the other accepted a bourbon cream. Tea and biscuits with chemo: there was something reassuringly, fabulously Irish about it.

Meanwhile, at home, I started putting soya milk in my coffee. Unfortunately coffee was also a big no-no, allegedly. Information that made it all the nicer. And I started gaining weight, which I put down to a combination of factors: being on steroids; the weird nausea-hunger that seemed to demand only one thing – carbs; the lure of easy-to-prepare meals, i.e., carbs; illness blues and 'Ah, I don't care' thinking, which resulted in one particular food group leaping to my lips – carbs. It was toast ahoy, potatoes hooray, pasta is faster than answering the question, 'What ought I really be eating?' The weigh-in before every chemo reminded me of WeightWatchers, with the weight steadily creeping up rather than down.

By weigh-in, on chemo three, 17 August, the scales

showed I had gained three and a half kilos since it had begun four weeks previously. I thought they'd said eight to ten pounds weight gain was to be expected over the course of chemo. Maybe that was kilos. I made a note to myself: 'Do remember, part of the weight-gain process does involve actually lifting, of one's own volition, carbs to the face area, and the voluntary opening of the mouth to allow insertion ...'

'I eliminated sugar, packaged food, dairy, alcohol, additives, and bought only organic produce,' a cancer blogger wrote.

'Oh, what does it matter? There's so much poison going into your body anyway,' was a fellow patient's attitude to the notion of radical diet change. Another said she couldn't eat because there was such a horrible taste 'of metal' in her mouth.

I never had such problems. 'Metastasis,' I noted in my diary. 'The word sounds to me like a plate of starters in a Lebanese restaurant.' The biggest issue I had with food was the night I decided to see what effect eating a chilli would have. I'd been warned to avoid hot and spicy dishes. A slice of green chilli lingered on my plate in the remains of a Chinese takeaway. ('Remains of a Chinese takeaway' – yes, that tells you everything about my commitment to a self-saving ultra-pure diet.) Since I didn't appear to be affected by the taste and appetite issues that plagued lots of others on chemo, I'd wondered how the chilli experience would affect me. Here's how. I might as well have gargled a cup of petrol and stuck a lighted match in my mouth. It wasn't anything like the normal experience of chilli heat: it was sheer pain. It hurt so much I was weeping with it. I ran into the kitchen to find something to salve it, as urgent as if my head was on fire – water made it worse, ditto milk, fruit juice, a measure of my prescribed oral fungicide, any liquid I could lay my hands on to try to ease the shocking hurt in my mouth. I was simultaneously aware of how pathetic my emergency situation was – 'Doctor, Doctor, cancer-treatment emergency! I was messing with chilli.' Natural yogurt did the trick in the end. Handy tip if you experience something similar: spoon natural yogurt into your gob, sit back, and feel truly ridiculous.

At any rate, I wasn't one of those women who lose their appetite.

10. Hair Here

There's a continuum of response to chemotherapy hair loss. At one end, people experience it like a woman who told me losing her hair was worse than losing her breast because, she said, it was more public. At the other, there are people who respond as my cousin Carmel did: 'It's one less thing to worry about. You just shower and go.' Or as I did, with 'Yippee! An unavoidable opportunity to see what I look like with a Sinéad O'Connor head.' When else, why else, would you shave your head – unless you were Sinéad O'Connor in one of her recurrent 'Actually, let's all forget what I said about retiring from the stage. I'm back, and I'm bald again to prove it' phases? As for it 'being public', personally I couldn't care two hoots. If I met people I knew and they said, 'What's up with the hair?' I replied, 'Cancer.' Why hide it? For me, open acknowledgement and sharing took the sting out of its tail. Big deal, I have cancer, so do so many.

And at the same time, it really is a big deal: I am newly dealing with having stage-three cancer so cut me some slack. Acknowledge my fabulous 'excuse'. I've got cancer, what's yours? The fact it was 'public' suited me, I discovered. Furthermore, I liked the way my shaved head looked. And even further furthermore, and perhaps most pertinently, I didn't have to hide the fact of my cancer for career, personal or family reasons. I felt lucky in that there was no pressure against letting it all hang out. Meanwhile, prior to becoming bald, I did what was suggested and got me a wig.

It's suggested you get your wig fitted while you've still got your usual hairstyle. 'What colour will my hair grow back?' I had asked the oncologist.

'The same colour it's dyed now,' he'd said.

'Not dyed,' I corrected, resisting the urge to add, 'Touché, Mr God.' My hair was shoulder length, dead straight, naturally dark brunette. Conversations with other cancer ladies confirmed it could grow back any which way, grey as sooty snow, curly, frizzy, wavy, kinked, or as was. So if you want your wig to mirror your hair as it is before treatment, get the wig before it has fallen away. Obvious point maybe, but in the maelstrom of that time, if it hadn't been pointed out to me, I would have headed to the wig shop only when bald.

My friend Sue, mother of four under seven, drove my sister and me to the wig place. I found it amusing, setting out on such a task in a people-carrier full of kids' seats, a car full of the absent buzz of young life. The wig shop was upstairs over a terraced row of shops in a south

Dublin suburb. I buzzed the bell by the low-key entrance a few times. 'Hello, I've an appointment,' I called into the intercom, when it was finally answered.

'The door's open!' the voice said.

Oh, yeah, so it was. What was I thinking? A place so discreet it must be locked against all-comers? Inside, bald sick women furtively trying on fake hair – 'Does the Afro suit me, Dolores, or will I stick with the shag?'

We were seated in a small fitting room, me in front of a large mirror, ready to be fitted with fake hair. We were given brochures to flick through. One featured the celebrity endorsement of Raquel Welch. The sexy movie star formerly famous for her ample bosoms, promoting hair replacement for women who in the main were being treated for breast cancer? I found that amusing. We assumed the fitting would take ages – there seemed so many possibilities now we were in the wig emporium. But I didn't go down the 'Sure now I'm here I might as well try everything. Who knows? Long wavy blonde may be the look that's been waiting for me my whole life' route, or succumb to the temptation of suggesting, 'You know what? I think I'd like to explore the possibilities of a Brian May.' Nope. The wig fitter came in with four sensible samples to match the natural on my head, and I went with her second suggestion. No messing. We, my sister, Sue and I, all thought it looked fabulous – at the time.

I was advised, when wearing it, to be careful of things like standing under those heaters they have in smoking areas outside pubs. It could melt. Top hint, I thought. No smirting (smoking and flirting) while on chemo. Imagine the embarrassment, out on the town, trying to chat up a lad by pretending to be a smoker, and next thing your hair is slowly dripping down your face, and he freaks 'cause he thinks you're a disguised alien, and how were you to know about his ketamine problem, and then he's trying to kill you with a beer mat, you're screaming for your life and it all gets a bit embarrassing ...

Yes, interesting information about the potentially melting wig, and a good job that two gifts of the cancer and chemotherapy are asexuality and anti-sociability, in my experience anyway. Outdoor heater: it wouldn't be a problem.

As well as wigs, there was a plethora of headgear on offer: elasticated jersey turbans and skull caps, marketed by pictures of wanly smiling women bobbing their heads at jaunty angles. All were the kind of bonce garment that screams, 'Hey, everybody, she's only wearing me because SHE'S GOT CANCER.' I bought one with a tied-to-the-side scarf effect. Funky, I thought – at the time. I never wore it: I was never in the fancy-dress-pirate-with-cancer kind of mood it seemed to suggest when I got it home and looked at it on my head, in the mirror, in the ordinary domestic setting.

Similarly, the wig became one of those what-was-I thinking purchases. 'What were we thinking?' I asked Sue.

'You were in a wig environment when you chose it,' was her take on the odd choice. 'You were surrounded by wigs. You tried it on, you were thinking, Wow, this looks so natural – compared to other wigs.' The lesson being, beware the muddying wigginess of the wig shop. Remember, you've got to work that thing on your head on Civvy Street. Also, you change as you go through treatment. Physically, mentally, you find yourself transformed. You may not think a reddish-brunette shaggy bob that looks like a country teacher's after a trip to the 'That's a grand do altogether' hairdresser suits you any more.

The next day I got my hair cropped short. The crop being the interim stage, before it all fell out. That meant less hair to be vacuumed around my apartment when it started to happen; it was an opportunity to experience what having 'dead short hair' looked like, before getting the opportunity to see what 'no hair' looked like, but it was expensive for a haircut that lasted just a few days. I went to my usual pricey hairdresser. And they refused to hear my invocation for a special one-off discount! 'I have breast cancer,' I told the stylist. 'I need my hair cropped because it's all going to fall out shortly. I've just started chemotherapy. The haircut you're going to give me is only going to last a couple of days. Did I mention I have breast cancer?'

'You can have a fiver off,' she said eventually.

Sixty-five euro for a three-day chop? I felt it undignified to start wailing, but did you hear me say cancer? If there was one way I sure hadn't lost the penchant for living, it was my everlasting beady eye for the bottom line. I fumed about the fiver discount. I'd made a mistake going on my own: I needed the presence of another to honour the significance of that visit to the salon. It mattered, and

I was discounting as much by going alone, as if it were nothing. Except I'd wanted a discount I didn't get. And I felt pathetically ratty about it, looking for an acknowledgement, some comfort, from some hair salon employee that I should have sought from those closest. My irritation that day was, in one psychotherapy word, transference.

Alone, I had to fight not to cry as my locks tumbled to the floor. Instead I focused on the fact that the 'Mia Farrow circa *Rosemary's Baby*' I was left with looked good. Plus I enjoyed leaving no tip.

'Will you be terribly annoyed if it doesn't fall out now?' my friend Michelle asked, when she saw the crop later that day.

No, I said, mainly because I knew there was no way that it was not going to fall out – 'All of it,' the oncologist had said, making no bones about it.

A few days after the chop, I noticed lots of stray hairs sticking to my skin when I was doing a hot yoga class. That's odd, still stray cuttings from the hairdresser, I thought, when I spotted the first few. Which you might call complete denial, because I'd washed my hair several times in the interim so how could it possibly have been stray cuttings? It was only, after a pose in which the upper arms press against the head, that I twigged: my arms came away covered with dark clippings. Then more and more appeared, peppered everywhere, on my towel, my chest, my legs when we did 'standing head to leg' pose. My hair was falling out. All of it. 'Don't cry, don't cry,' I told myself. Nobody notices when you cry in Bikram yoga anyway: the tears look like sweat.

I phoned my sister when I got home. She came round with a video camera and we made a ridiculous stop-motion video of me pulling out my hair, then sticking it back on with Pritt, laughing uncontrollably as we went. And then she started weeping when she saw the bald patch left on the top of my head, the vulnerable stark soft white of scalp skin contrasted with the thick surrounding dark hair. That was all falling out.

'Does it burn off or fall out?' Someone posted a query about chemo hair loss on a cancer chat room. What? Does chemo somehow sear your scalp and gradually your head starts to smoulder? That's not chemo: that's being on the ground during a US air attack in the Vietnam War. It just comes away, like in a bad dream. You tug, and out it comes, in clumps. Strands of it were shedding all round my flat. It splattered my bathtub, strands of black on white, when I showered.

A trick of my own: I got masking tape, stuck and ripped it in strips all over my head, trying to ease off the excess. I was left with a lovely souvenir of that crazy time: reams of hairy tape, which I saved, with all sorts of other cancer-treatment knick-knacks – if one day I wanted to make an art installation of it, it'd be there, not discarded as the rubbish it was. My inspiration was the medical-inspired art pieces I'd seen in my last exhibition, the weekend before I was diagnosed: the Tracey Emin retrospective at the Hayward Gallery in London.

Two to three weeks, the oncologist had said. It was almost two weeks to the day since my first chemo, my second was the morning following that sudden shedding.

I had called the wig salon and booked in to get my hair totally shaved off that afternoon – a complimentary service they offered with the wig fitting. 'It's more private here than a hairdresser's,' the assistant had said.

I was interested to see what I would look like. 'At least you've got the face for it,' my friend Gene commented. 'You've got big eyes – if you had narrow little slitty ones you'd look like a lizard.'

Watching someone run an electric trimmer over your scalp, watching part of your identity tumble in a dark rain on the floor, is ... odd. Negative on the one hand, so many resonances, prisoners, victims of war, English townswoman who's fallen in love with a German soldier during the Second World War. But on the other hand it was dead positive: I loved the look.

The wig had cost a whopping four hundred and something euro. It looked very natural although it was synthetic, easier to maintain than a real-hair wig, according to the fitter. But when I saw my bare head, I thought, This looks much funkier.

There were comments. 'Hey, Baldy,' a drunk young man shouted at me in a Dart station one evening. 'Baldy! You!' he repeated, when I paid him no heed.

'I've got cancer,' I bellowed back, down the rail platform.

'Hey, man, respect, my dad died of cancer,' he shouted back. A heartening cancer experience: love from junkies.

Another evening, cycling along Dublin's quays, a bunch of kids shouted, 'Look, it's Jade Goody,' after me. Another heartening cancer experience: chirpy commentary from ruffians.

'What do you think of this?' I asked an artist I know at the opening of the huge Dublin Contemporary Art Exposition 2011.

'Bald really suits you,' she said.

'No,' I said. 'I meant the exhibition.'

Back in yoga, a classmate enquired if I was going to wear a wig at all. I told her I wasn't because I didn't want to miss out on any of the whole 'I've got cancer' experience. 'I know what you mean,' she said. 'You'll meet someone, they'll say, "I've got a terrible flu," and you can go, "I'll see your flu, and raise you a cancer."' Exactly.

'What happened to your hair?' one of the Pakistani assistants asked in my local shop.

'I'm on chemo,' I said.

'Yes, chemo, I understand,' he replied gravely. His colleague wanted to know what that was. He explained, adding to me, 'My father was on that. He had throat cancer.'

'And how is he now?' I asked.

'He's dead,' he replied.

'You look better with no hair,' a friend's five-year-old commented. 'It's so cheerful.'

Out of the mouths of babes ... It was nice to know I had a cheerful head.

And I made my wig cheerful too, by relegating it to use onstage with The Nualas.

11. Nuala

It happened in a kitchen, the room where I always end up at parties, in Drumcondra, a north Dublin suburb. As our official PR biography puts it: 'In May 1995, The Nualas were formed when Susan Collins, Tara Flynn and Anne Gildea got together over the leftovers at a party. Their mutual love of food, comedy and singing inspired them to form a trio and book their first ten-minute slot. At that first gig, they brought the house down and as they crawled out of the comedy rubble that night they knew they were destined for great things.'

I knew Sue because she was dating my brother at the time, and Tara from hacking around the Dublin comedy scene. They were actresses who were also involved in comedy improvisation. Finding ourselves alone in the kitchen at a house party, we started improvising songs together. In a Hollywood-type 'Hey, let's put on a show' moment, we decided to meet the following week to write songs.

We wrote three, the first, 'Manolo', about a Spanish lover man who turns out to be from Ballymun: 'When

I left Claremorris my hymen was intact/After only one sangria you were on me like a jack rabbit.' We called ourselves The Nualas because the name 'Nuala' evoked a strong, sensible, grounded country woman, the type who might be a nurse or a lovely air hostess. It wasn't a name you'd instantly associate with pop superstardom.

The premise of The Nualas was that we were three farm girls who were in an international supergroup, three lassies as comfortable on a Zetor tractor as sipping cocktails with Steven Seagal. It was just before the Spice Girls exploded. And just before Ireland started hotting up as a modern economy. The image of Ireland as the poor mutt of Europe, shivering in Atlantic isolation off the far edge of the continent, was about to be supplanted by Ireland, one of the richest, at the centre of stuff. We were on the cusp of becoming that stripy beast of economic miracle – the Celtic Tiger. The Nuala element, us as no-nonsense celebs, sophist (rural short-hand for sophisticated) farm girls, superstars with cow manure on our fancy shoes, bits of silage stuck between our sequins and a don't-mess-with-us up-for-the-craic vibe, was perfect for the times that were in it. That it hit those zeitgeisty notes was pure coincidence – a happy accident that it had come together and worked. Writing, performing and promoting the act was, from the word go, like pushing an open door.

Two weeks after getting together we performed as The Nualas for the first time, and got our first press mention, from that night, in *Hot Press*, the Irish music paper: 'First on, though, are The Nualas, a deranged Wilson Phillips to cut out and keep.' Having trawled around doing so much

that had never quite worked before The Nualas, I knew
we'd happened upon something really special.

I was Upbeat Nuala, as my biography for a tour
programme goes:

> Nuala's family weren't well off – often a trotter and
> a cabbage would be boiled on a Monday morning,
> and it would have to do them until Tuesday …
> fortnight. Times were hard. The family longed for
> a proper roof over their heads, instead of a carpet
> held up by vaulting poles (their uncle was a gymnast
> in America and they would receive a long package
> every winter), and many's the time Nuala and her
> brothers and sisters were ridiculed at school for the
> holes in their boots, gymslips, trousers and blazers,
> which were all made out of bin bags. But they silently
> agreed as long as their father was happy down in
> Dolan's pub every morning, noon and bastarding
> night, they didn't mind. They survived.
>
> Oh yes indeed, Nuala survived. Upbeat loves
> her now glamorous touring lifestyle, skipping from
> B&B to B&B, belting out self-penned classics and
> being lauded by packed houses of up to fifty-eight
> people plus. But as Upbeat sits in her dressing
> room, smoking a cheroot and sipping her Scrumpy
> Jack, she knows she'll never get too big for her
> boots (which are no longer made out of bin bags
> but out of dead ponies). Invariably at moments like

these the often repeated slurred words of her father
spring to mind –
    'Always remember, you're absolutely crap.'

Extraordinary things happened. For example, shortly after getting together, we were chatting together over supper in a restaurant, prior to doing a gig in the Baggot Inn, a Dublin venue. We were having a debate as to whether or not to go to the Edinburgh Fringe Festival on spec to play whatever gigs we could muster and see what interest there might be in the UK. We decided we couldn't afford to. After our performance that evening a chap approached us, said he'd thought we were wonderful, that he'd overheard our conversation in the restaurant, and we simply must go to Edinburgh. So he was going to fund it. He took my address. Next day he knocked on my door, handed me three flight tickets to Scotland, and a bank card for withdrawing funds when we got there. We went, we slept on floors, we trawled the streets, guitar in hand, playing gigs wherever there was a stage and a few students. We ended up with a slot at the notoriously rowdy *Late and Live Show* in the main theatre of the Gilded Balloon venue, and got an encore. That night the venue's producer, Karen Koren, offered us a run in a hundred-and-fifty-seat venue for the following year.

Back home, after Edinburgh, our show in the first Dublin Fringe Festival was a huge hit, and was picked up by a commercial theatre venue for a Christmas run; a telly appearance on an arts show led to a slot on RTÉ's prime-time *Late Late Show*, and thus began a trajectory we sustained for our group's initial seven years together.

Our Edinburgh Festival theatre runs led to a series with BBC Radio 4; we toured Australia and headlined the first Singapore Comedy Festival. We were booked for a special two-act extended set on the first series of BBC TV's *The Stand Up Show*, sharing the bill with US stand-up Jon Stewart. London's *Time Out* said, 'Two longer sets from two significantly better-than-usual acts.' We had sold-out theatre runs in London, had a summer season in the Dublin Tivoli Theatre that extended to nine weeks; we played all the grand old houses, Dublin's Olympia and Gaiety Theatres, Cork and Belfast's Opera Houses, and did a sixty-five-date tour of the UK that culminated in London's Royal Albert Hall with an evening of Irish acts for the North/South charity Co-operation Ireland – where afterwards, odd showbiz memory, somebody told us, 'David Trimble said you were the best.'

To give an idea of who The Nualas were, here's a 'typical day', as described, in character, for an Irish newspaper to promote the run we did at the Tivoli Theatre in 1999:

The alarm usually goes off at 7.30 a.m. – that's because it's faulty. We usually get up at mid-day, depending on what we're doing. For instance, if we're shooting a video we have to get up earlier, 11.30 or so. We're very flexible – you have to be in this business we call show.

Usually we have a rasher and sausage breakfast, with omelettes, toast and chops on the side. Tea features big-time in all our diets. Big pots of tea. Yum. We usually listen to Pat Kenny when we get up – just to keep with the cutting edge.

We all live and work together – so that solves the problem of commuting. Our typical working day involves chat, arguments, vocal exercises, tea, guitar lessons, biscuits, brain storming and automatic writing. Of course, while we're doing the run in the Tivoli all of the above will be replaced by sleep.

Fidelma, our personal assistant, handles all our phone calls, emails, faxes, letters and bouquets. She's also a trained sniper, in case we're having trouble with the stalkers.

If we go out for lunch we usually like to try out somewhere bijou and sophist, with big portions – like the RTÉ canteen. We'll often share a *coq au vin* with Marian or Pat out there – we can stick it on the *Kenny Live* tab.

We love everything about living in Dublin, except the traffic, air, litter, rent, concrete, clamping and the price of stuff. To relax we go upstairs in Renards and hang out with other celebs over a couple of Red Bulls and a cocktail sausage. If we're in a party mood we'll go to Joys on Baggot Street. There's a super gang of back-bench TDs who hang out there – great craic and real gentlemen: they always pick up the tab for the Blue Nun at the end of the night.

If we're staying in for the evening we're quite

particular about what TV programmes we watch on telly. Generally we only watch news programmes, documentaries, current-affairs discussions and *Beverly Hills, 90210*. We read a broad range of newspapers – anything that has any mention of us in it. And, of course, being in showbiz, we subscribe to all the trades – *What Hi-Fi*, *Smash Hits*, *Gigs Ahoy!*, etc. etc. It's important to keep in touch and not get locked in the insulated limo of your fame – Chris de Burgh told us that.

Our songs ran the gamut from funky ballad to less funky ballad, exhibited in this short selection of titles and descriptions: 'Bridget the Nun', stomping tale of a cycling sister; 'Brittany Baskerville', in the tradition of Jacques Brel and Rolf Harris, a song about someone from the bog prancing around in a diamond bikini; 'Curly Kay', a jazz number about a generous girl, with a cabbage for a head, who gets lost in one of Europe's most interesting ecosystems; 'Fares Please', a poppy ballad about a romantic occurrence on an element of the public transportation network and its most delicate and beautiful development therein; 'Flatmates', a jazz essay about splitting the rent with eejits; 'The Medley', in the great tradition of jamming a few songs together and calling it a new song; 'Moan', a rock-out protest song, featuring descant recorder.

In between there was what *Time Out* called the 'artfully wry banter'. Below an *ad-hoc* example, some show-opening banter from back in the day:

NUALA 1: Well, it's been a big week in politics. England is now part of Ireland. Articles Two and Three of the Constitution are now Four and Five inclusive. A packet of cigarettes is now ten punts. And it's been a great time for Irish housewives. Don't think your work has gone unnoticed – because it has.

NUALA 2: Jackie Collins has been commissioned to write the first volume of Jeffrey Archer's biography – *Dirty Shitbag Slutty Liar: the early years*.

NUALA 3: And this next number is an a capella song, dedicated to a man I met last night. Malachy, I seem to remember he said his name was. Malachy Mulcahy from 46b McCurtain Street. You got one honour in your Leaving Cert, you work as a freelance butcher and your father's a priest – I've got all the relevant details and if you don't come backstage after the gig and make arrangements for maintenance payments you'll be hearing from my lawyer. Thanks very much indeed, Malachy.

Our final run was in the Irish Arts Center in New York. We'd been due to open on 12 September 2001, but Irish actor/comic Niall Tóibín took that slot with his one-man show instead, and the rest, as they say, was a run that didn't happen for him because of the events of 9/11. We opened on 2 October. A positive review in the *New York Times* meant we extended from three to seven weeks. Doors were suddenly opening, just we were closing the

Leabharlanna Poibli Chathair Bhaile Átha Cliath
Dublin City Public Libraries

door on us. One of the many whys that come up in Nuala interviews: why did you disband after such a successful US début, after so much hard work getting there? I can see that it seems idiotic, but the single one-word answer is, burnout. Sue and I were just thoroughly frazzled from the constant touring, the ups and downs of four line-up changes.

That's another: why all the line-up changes? The curse of the trio, somebody once said to Sue. I think it was Jesus, in a dream. There's not much more to say about it other than, as Sue's character used to say on stage, *'Non, je ne regrette rien* – no, I can't remember anything.' Luckily Sue and I always had the desire to keep The Nualas on the road. Her Nuala was totally no-nonsense, hence her name, No-nonsense Nuala. As our programme notes once described her: '"Down to earth and practical" are her middle names. She's as comfortable throwing a brick through a vivisectionist's window as she is lounging on her *chaise longue* in a mink negligée.'

A last why: why didn't ye make it bigger? Well, it seemed we were on the cusp of lucrative things many a time: the cusp of getting something major on telly; the cusp of major international catwalk modelling careers, the cusp of getting a huge advertising campaign – and one of them isn't true.

As a window into how big things don't happen, this is the story of us nearly getting a Major Advertising Campaign, some time in the late 1990s. It involves a brewery that shall remain nameless, except to say that it was based in Cork.

THE NUALAS GO MAD WITH MAD MEN

First off, it must be said that, generally, two things need to be borne in mind when offered the opportunity to sell your creativity for the advertising buck.

1. Advertising is evil. It exists to breed the dissatisfaction that creates the consumption that oils the cogs of the global economy that's heading us towards the destruction of our environment in particular, and life on earth in general.

2. It pays well.

Once upon a time a brewery came a-calling, looking for The Nualas to front a major campaign: telly ads, radio ads, posters, personal appearances, tour funding, the whole banana. Our first meeting was a late-nighter because Ding-Dong (not his real name), the art director of the proposed campaign, had just flown in from New York. We met in a conference room of one of the better Dublin hotels. It was just a 'hello' meeting. 'Hello,' we said, and they, Ding-Dong, his assistant, also fresh in from the States, the man from the brewery and the PR person responded in kind. Then we drank a lot of very expensive wine and hung around long enough to ensure we were all *on the same page, singing from the same hymn sheet* and fit to choke on the smoke from the brewery man's Cubans (this was a while ago, when people were allowed to do their lung-cancer thang indoors).

Next was dinner in one of the better Dublin restaurants. As we slugged the finest wines available to humanity, talk was of water: liquid, for yachting, wind-surfing and owning property near, and frozen, for skiing and snowboarding. 'Do you have any hobbies, Anne?' Ding-Dong suddenly enquired.

'Paddling and snowballs,' I lied, to fit in.

It worked. At the end of the evening we were all *speaking the same language, riding the same wave, bouncing from the same bungee.*

Then it was time for work. We convened around a conference table in an even better Dublin hotel than the last. Ding-Dong held a pointy stick and stood beside his top-of-the-range flipchart. 'We're thinking something like this,' he said, flipping and tapping. He'd done some pretty fancy graphics.

'I like the look of that,' I said, to be positive.

'These are just mock-ups,' he said. 'The final thing won't look like this at all.'

'So what are they?'

'They're just to show you.'

To show what, I'm still not sure. But I suppose he had to be doing something to make his trip worthwhile. We looked at many more designs that would have absolutely nothing to do with the final campaign, but we were all given an idea of something. We flung around a few more ideas, ate some up-market sandwiches and then it was time for Ding-Dong to leave. He had to be home to tuck his daughter into bed that night. In Connecticut.

He didn't want to miss his Concorde (a while ago, as I said). His assistant, who, according to what I'd heard, had never said anything, left with him. She wasn't on the same plane. None of us were, for that matter. We never met again.

It goes without saying, the campaign never happened.

December 2001, back from New York, we did two farewell gigs in Dublin's Olympia Theatre. Having some space away from all the Nualadom-intensity was great – for about six years. Then longing set in to be back on that glittery girl-group pony again, riding around the field of glamorous international showbiz dressage. In other words, eventually I missed the three Cs the group had provided: cash, company and craic. And the two Fs: fun and fame. And the double S: some security. And a W: work. And a big fat I: identity. I'd done many things in the interim, worked on Irish telly, radio and as a comedy tour producer. I'd gone back to stand-up and done solo shows. I had published a novel, and become a newspaper columnist. But there was a space left in all of that which could only be filled by putting on the sequined wellies of our girl group again.

I spent a couple of years nagging No-nonsense Nuala Sue, who, meanwhile, had become mum-of-many. Finally, she had a tiny window in her crazy schedule, and she cracked. She had been on the verge of having a sitcom she'd co-written developed by BBC 1. At the last, it didn't happen. The ultimate deciding factor for our reunion was the sudden possibility of a good Irish TV offer for The Nualas. Ultimately that didn't happen either but what did was better – The Nualas were back together. November 2010, after much hunting, a new third Nuala was captured: Maria Tecce, a Bostonian singer and musician. Musical Father Dougal Nuala we christened her, and it was all go again.

This was an interview I did at the time, as Nuala, promoting and explaining our return to the stage:

What took you so long to reunite – and why now?

Call it a 'showbiz technicality': if you don't leave it a while before you 'reunite' it's not a 'reunite' any more, is it? It's more of an 'Oh, look, it's them. Are they still going round and round?' Right now felt like the right time 'cause there's so many raggedy old groups trying to get back together – Take That, The Stone Roses, Fianna Fáil. We're just going with the flow, really.

What can we expect from your new show?

All the old favourite hits, some of the ancient ones, and fabulous new material addressing contemporary concerns, like the harsh economic climate; love in the harsh economic climate; and shoulder pads – right or wrong in a harsh economic climate? Plus glamour, harmony, shiny dresses and a special instrumental on a musical saw – and three ladies wearing similar lipstick who all look like they enjoy chips quite often, all called Nuala.

What shouldn't we expect?

Nudity, juggling, chorus lines, anyone being
referred to as 'Pegeen Mike' or 'Fluther' or 'Babby-
Bobby', big reels, uilleann pipes, rabbits out of hats,
an orchestra, pole-dancing, anyone pretending
to be Spider Man flying on wires over you in the
audience, and crashing into a multi-million-dollar
stage set, resulting in concussion and broken arms
and legs and wrists, and delays and legal actions,
and / or anything less than three experienced ladies
all called Nuala singing in very close harmony about
things that you didn't know mattered so much to
you until you heard them being sung about in very
close harmony by a trio of showbiz goddesses all
called Nuala – basically.

*What's your strongest memory of your first ever Nualas
gig?*

Nuala's boyfriend at the time – Pat 'Biceps' McPecs
O'Bench-Press.

*What is the most bizarre moment you've had in your
showbiz experience?*

When we went to see another show on tour, and
Nuala got hypnotised, got up on stage as a dog
– and the most humiliating thing was that it was
during a production of *Hamlet*.

What's the oddest place – or audience – you've ever

experienced while touring as The Nualas?

We once played a 'Trio Conference' in Nashville – and there were only two people in the audience.

Are there Nualas groupies out there?

Well, there's often a man at my garden gate, shouting, 'Please, let me into your life, Nuala. I love the ground your FitFlops walk upon.' But he's also an ex-husband of mine, so does that count?

Have you ever had a proper job?

You could say no. In the great Irish tradition, like so many before – Sean Fitzpatrick, David Drumm, Patrick Neary, Bertie Ahern, Sean Dunne, Brian Cowen and on and on, and so, so, so many others – you could say we were inexorably attracted to the shiny world of make-believe.

What did you want to be when you grew up?

Taller.

If you had a kangaroo's pouch what would you keep in it?

Heaps of subordinated bonds.

We played Vicar Street. We booked a tour. We were back. Four months later I was in treatment for cancer.

12. I'm Every Woman

If you were going through cancer treatment, would you be worried about toning down that steroid-flushed complexion? Counteracting that facial puffiness? Blushing up that mid-chemo-cycle pallor, bringing out your sunken eyes, teasing that ol' wig to its synthetic optimum? No. I wasn't particularly either. But I jumped at the opportunity to attend a workshop addressing such matters, when it was mentioned to me by the hospital social worker. Well – 'jumped' probably isn't the right word.

I had had four counselling sessions with her – four hours of me sobbing in her office, apologising, 'I'm sorry, you must have to deal with so much of this', while going with the fact that it was the only space I wanted to allow such an expression of what the illness, and its concomitant offshoots, felt like. I didn't feel the need to cry like that with anyone else, but it was a relief to let it out, to access that well of ongoing shock-emotion that still needed tearful draining; a relief to cry with a professional witness, too, however much I didn't want to feel I was 'dumping'.

Anyway, I blubberingly said, 'Yep,' at her mention of the workshop. 'Look Good, Feel Better', it was called. The concept had originated in the United States, a complementary service for female cancer patients, offering makeup advice to those feeling overwhelmed by the change in their appearance while going through treatment. In Ireland it's organised and funded by the Cancer Society.

It might be nice, soppy-me admitted, although the deeper socio-historic-feminist-perspective me protested, *Oh, for God's sake!* Is my lower-caste Indian sister festering to her cancerous death on a slum street in Kolkata worried about the state of her eyeliner and bindi? Were medievals with plague protesting about powdering their noses before being tossed on the death cart? Are men doing it? Nope, no special workshop get-togethers for men that I heard of – light DIY for those afflicted in the man-sac: 'Make Yourself Useful, Feel Better'.

Wasn't it a bit retrograde and patronising to suggest, come on, ladies, you being ladies, there's nothing like a bit of slap to lift those chemotherapy spirits? My default guideline for being adequately turned out during chemotherapy was, if you don't smell, you're OK. Plus a bit of lipstick, if you can be arsed. It wasn't much different from my usual attitude. 'My ex-wife was always very well groomed,' my last ex had said.

'What are you trying to tell me?' I asked him. 'That she was a horse?'

Oh, how he didn't laugh.

In a nut, the idea of Look Good, Feel Better riled me slightly: bombarded up to our cancerous chests by images of what women should be, why can't we let up on it even when we're afflicted with something that could very well kill us? Why can't we allow ourselves be in the moment we're in? Time out! That was what *my* body was saying. I needed the world to cut me some slack, some space to be sick, not to feel I had to put a painted face on it.

In that context, a bit of me felt like going, 'Do not insult me with your suggestion of lippy and blusher, foundation and powder puff.' But then again, I'd got wind of the fact that all the cosmetics were complimentary. Hey, what was not to love? Free shit, I was in.

Yes, the idea may have seemed as offbeat to me as 'Fashion Tips for Lepers', or 'Macaroons for the Malnourished', but I swallowed my reservations, and took my lovely big white bespoke Look Good, Feel Better cosmetics sack – with its liners, blushers, pencils, lippy, foundation, a cream for taking down the red glow of meds on your face and a Jean Paul Gaultier perfume, called, appositely enough, 'Fragile'.

There were twelve of us at the workshop, women at various stages of treatment for various types of cancer but mainly breast. We sat around a large conference table, in a squashy room in the hospital's social-work prefab. There were little propped-up makeup mirrors for each of us, our individual complimentary makeup bags beside them. For some reason I was reminded of something my mother used to tell me when I was a kid: it's a sin to look in the mirror.

A woman at the head of the table showed us how to do stuff we all pretty much knew inside out anyhow. With some new hints I'd never heard before, like 'When you're putting on foundation, squirt it on the side of your hand, so it doesn't get absorbed into the palm.' Oh? The girl seated beside me was twenty-seven years old; she had oestrogen positive breast cancer, was coming to the end of eight rounds of chemotherapy, after which she would be having a double mastectomy.

There was the trick to drawing the perfect brow, when there's no hair left to guide where the line goes. I was waiting for our instructor to go, 'And remember, ladies, eyebrow over the eye!' Why, oh why, was I so curmudgeonly? Chemo fatigue? I really wasn't feeling terribly well that day.

Or was it something deeper? Yes – simply, I've always been uncomfortable with being told, as a woman, what you were supposed to be like, to do, to want. It goes right back to being a kid, to all the first things learned about being a woman. Things I got mad fiery about later, when the scales fell from my eyes and I put on my feminista-goggles.

It started with the Playtex 18-hour girdle, on telly – those ads when I was a child, impressionable and wide-eyed about what being a woman entailed. According to these mini-films of startling information, it meant wearing massive thick knickers that went from above the knee all the way up to becoming a huge big bra that crossed your heart, and gave you a bust like twin conical warheads. Those ladies on telly, wearing nothing but these big smalls and makeup, admired themselves in the mirror, smoothing their hands down over their held-in bellies, with smiles on their lipsticked mouths that told you in their heads they were saying, 'WOW!' They were supposed to be over the moon because those big knickers wouldn't hurt that much for up to eighteen hours. Why they should hurt at all wasn't a question. Binding yourself in elasticated fabric, was, I thought when I was a kid, the very definition of feminine maturity. Men in ads on telly weren't in big elasticated knickers. Why not? You didn't even think to ask. It was just the way it was. Men smoked panatellas, slugged beer and said, 'Ah, that's Bass' and eyed up women, especially if they'd bothered to put on the hurty undies. And women showed themselves off in those undies, and looked absolutely delighted about it.

Then there was the chiffon-scarf test ad. I thought that was something you'd be doing as a matter of course when you grew up. You'd be getting dressed, you'd have got as far as putting on your slip, and then you'd think, Hang on, stop. I'd better put my leg up on a chair here, before I pull on my nylons, and test myself. And you'd let a flimsy scarf slip down the leg, and if it caught on anything, you were in the wrong. You hadn't used Immac hair-removal stuff. If you had, the scarf would have slid off your leg as if it was made of plastic, like Barbie's – which was exactly what you'd be after when you grew up. It wasn't clear who, other than yourself, would ever be conducting this test. But you'd be doing it just to be on the safe side.

(An advantage of the chemo: not a follicle remained on the body. Extreme waxer, eat your heart out. I didn't so much have a Brazilian or a Hollywood. It was more an Antarctica.)

The only other kind of telly women I remember from then were ones who'd succeeded in being slim, pretty and smooth enough to deserve being pinched on the bum by funny men in comedy programmes: 'Bombshells' who dropped in with the tray of tea, their explosive chests blowing the funny men's minds, from the comedy looks on their leery male faces. That was the way the men in funny films looked at women's chests, with a mixture of fear and funniness, before they got on with being the funny ones.

Then there were all the magazines, elucidating how to be a woman, every one of my mother's that I recall a schizophrenic mish-mash of lovely family recipes juxtaposed with dieting advice. Dinner menus and cakes for every occasion and reminders to be slim at the same time, and also, be warned, use moisturiser morning and night. To be a woman was to be a great cook, thin and soft. It was a struggle being all three – which was why it was always being banged on about. That was my mum, always struggling with the weight, always baking, her hands semi-soft at the end of it. One and a half out of three ain't bad.

My mum had a sheaf of recipes cut out and kept from magazines when she'd first got married, in the early sixties in England. I remember one was a spread featuring Harry Secombe's wife, explaining his favourite cakes. In the accompanying photos the portly Harry, a superstar comedian/entertainer of the era, scoffed the buns. His wife beamed in her pinny, amid arrays of her bakery, and as I recall there were some children in the picture. She: mother, cook, pamperer of Harry. He: star. I wanted to be the man bit of that equation, even as I followed the woman's tips for her perfect fudge icing.

Funny that, years later, involved in comedy, I noticed the principle of woman as 'person in background providing support' still going strong. Woman as homemaker bearing the kids, who provide ample joke-content, or groupie comfort, or agent or manager, roles proportionately much more female in comedy than actually being in front of the microphone.

'The way to a man's heart is through his stomach,' my mum oft repeated to me. To read women's magazines now you figure maybe she was aiming too high. But she reassured me that I'd never have a problem with men because she'd taught me to lash up any of ten different varieties of sponge cake quicker than you could say 'The chicken's in the oven.'

I was Mummy's little helper, becoming adept at every activity involving those top-brand housewife accessories of the time: Pledge, Windolene, Vim, Brillo pads and mild green Fairy Liquid. We might have been living in a slow chaos of disintegration, but I was taught to control what I could – the shine on the sideboard. Any bit of furniture that could be buffed, I grew up making it gleam. That was being good.

Long term, it turned me off the kitchen and the cleaning cupboard. If that sounds like a grand excuse for being a slob, believe me, it is. As an adult I discovered I was with

Joan Rivers on the monotony of housework: 'You make the beds, you do the dishes, and six months later you have to start all over again.'

I discovered feminist theory when I went to college in 1984. It was an intellectual orgasm of recognition. My God almighty, the way patriarchal society, with its ideological arm, the Church, and enforcing arm, the Law, and sneaky cultural arm, telly, ads and women's magazines, has trounced the rights of women, defined us as less, other, inferior, as property, as weak, unclean, frivolous, hairy, fat, not funny – et cetera, et cetera, et cetera. Marriage, raising kids, sexy dresses, high heels, being a dab hand at baking buns: were they just the badges of being the spare rib? I took that question to heart. Was I also deep down dead angry about past unhappiness, and was the theory a handy package for that too? A flaming outlet? For sure – I was angry about everything.

'Anne, clothes maketh the woman,' my mum would say to me, when I'd visit her in England. She had moved back to Manchester after she and my father had separated so I'd take the boat and train to visit her during college holidays. Yeah, yeah, I'd think, in my uniform of jeans and desert boots, combat jacket, second-hand men's shirts and baggy jumpers.

'I always thought you were a lesbian,' a college classmate I met years later said.

Mother was right-ish about the clothes. Yeah, on the one hand you didn't want to be pinned by the objectifying 'male gaze' that you were reading about; on the other, you did, a bit, for sex.

Now I look at students out on the town in Dublin and marvel that things have swung so far in the other direction. The notion of the objectifying male gaze is never mentioned any more, just visible everywhere as female fashion choice.

It wasn't that I lived the rest of my adult life in dungarees, cultivating an eco-system of body hair on my totally cosmetic-free, natural, anti-patriarchal lady-skin. I'd even tried Botox once, for an article, but my main interest was personal, to see if it would 'do anything' for me. I'd spent a lifetime looking at my wobbly body in the mirror and tutting in disgust. And, though I was fascinated by the negative sexual politics of the high shoe, still there was a heap of heels in the house I couldn't move in. And a wardrobe full of tops cut low to show off the cleavage I used to be proud of and delighted for a male eye to admire ...

But the woman I essentially was remained ever suspicious of yokes promoted as womanly passions: the glossies, *Sex and the City*, the fetishising of shoes and stupid handbags, interest in models, labels and what's coming off the catwalk. As I once wrote in a column on the topic:

I feel flawed, flabby, lacking adequate fabulous shoes, cool coats, nail polishes, co-ordinated separates and that time-old biggie, Sex Appeal. Me, who hasn't got so much a 'muffin top' as a veritable sponge-bod. Who last bought a handbag five years ago, and it cost a tenner. Who wishes there were bras out there that came with lifetime guarantees. Am I sub-human, a woman at all, or from a parallel universe? Or have I just been reading a stack of glossy women's fashion magazines and am now suffering the consequences? It's the latter. I came across a survey statistic recently that revealed, after reading glossies, 82 per cent of women feel 95 per cent worse about themselves – or something like that. And now I'm 100 per cent proof.

Yet the upshot was, I'd always felt, fundamentally, that I wasn't like Other Women. That somehow I was always outside the gang of ladies in general. Then I got breast cancer: the lurgy of the lovely motherly mammaries, the most feminine of illnesses. Women organise around it, have fun runs, charity lunches, cake sales, paddle big mad-looking dragon boats together because of it (the dynamic of such rowing is an exercise proven to reduce post-mastectomy lymphoedema), and, yes, have makeup afternoons to reconnect with the femininity they may feel is eroded when they're in the throes of treatment.

To be part of such things brought a comfort I'd rarely ever felt in being ordinarily feminine.

Breast cancer made me one of the gals. And I'm sure, like the other women attending the Look Good, Feel Better event that day, it was the shared experience I sought, rather than eyebrow advice.

13. A Taxol-ing Time

Dexamethasone. That was the name of the anti-inflammatory, immunosuppressant steroid tablets I took with chemotherapy. One of the more obscure pieces of information I discovered in my ongoing web binge is that dexamethasone is used illicitly by Bangladeshi prostitutes because it helps counteract the appearance of being malnourished. It turns an already robust Western ladybody into something of a human Puffa jacket, if you're me.

But, from the hospital's point of view, the main concern with the tablets wasn't weight gain but mood change. My sister had happened to mention to the oncologist that I seemed a bit 'high', the first time I took them. I guess that was a concern because when the chemotherapy switched from A/C to Taxol, a higher dose of those steroids came into play. On the A/C it was 32mg over the following two days. For Taxol, it would be 40mg taken over a few hours, half 'n' half, night and morning before treatment.

If the dose of A/C made you 'high' you could be stratospheric on Taxol.

So it was their prerogative to keep an eye out in case you turned into crazy lady – going on spending sprees, rewiring the house in the middle of the night: those were the kind of erratic potential behaviours I heard mentioned. I figured it didn't concern me because by A/C three the steroids just seemed to give me enough extra oomph to be functional; sprees and DIY were off my radar. I had no buzz to wreck by counteractive meds. But, a golden rule I discovered, be careful of any utterance your sister Una makes, to your oncologist.

On 17 August 2011, just before my third A/C treatment, it was strongly suggested to me that I should take the medication that would counteract the highs I was apparently hitting on dexamethasone. I was given a prescription for same. I said, no, thank you, I don't need them. That didn't go down too well, initially. What good was my take on what was happening in my own head? That, I felt, was the official medical view on my refusal to take the proffered medication. My perception might be coming from a perspective of me being up, and away in my gorgeous dexamethasone balloon.

I knew, from the ground of my own experience, that it wasn't so. The final outcome was that after some toing and froing, my non-compliance in this instance was accepted, but the whole incident really shook me up.

'You should see your relationship with the medical-care providers as a partnership,' a hospital professional I discussed the incident with later told me. Her point: that the patient should dynamically, not passively, engage with their medical treatment.

'Remember you're involved in a system,' another healthcare worker friend told me, 'people operating within a strict, large and very hierarchical organisational framework. So, necessarily you're going to be in situations where you'll have to defend your own needs, your own corner, against the sometimes perhaps inadvertently inappropriate onslaught of the automatic, systematic response.' Always, in other words, have a sense of taking responsibility for yourself.

When I look back, I think I was feeling slightly childlike up to then, overwhelmed by the diagnosis, wanting to feel unquestioningly safe and secure in the hospital, pathetically open and therefore unquestioningly, happily, allowing myself be buffeted along by the organisational automatic procedures. Like hospital was the loving arms of an all-knowing, love-flowing mammy, not an institution that, though expert in medical-care provision and 'caring', in as much as that was part of such provision, impartially embodied values, a culture, rules and guidelines that may sometimes clash with one's own boundaries.

'Boundaries': that was the key word. Having a 'Hold your horses, I'm not going to do what you're telling me to do right now' moment was a good wake-up call. Just because you have cancer, and find yourself suddenly, extraordinarily, swept into a (thankfully available) system focused on your treatment and survival does not mean you can drop all the boundaries you've developed to negotiate ordinary life.

Maybe that's a no-brainer for many, but part of me just wanted to be taken care of. I'd felt so uncertain and unsafe in my ordinary life, prior to the hospital adventure cancer involved.

The lesson was one of assertion.

On 14 September I had the first of the four Taxol treatments. And my mega steroids started. I'd been warned I probably wouldn't sleep after taking the tablets. Swallowing 20mg of dexamethasone at bedtime is like dropping an E, hoovering a couple of lines of nose candy, downing a Red Bull, then jumping into bed, and expecting excellent beddy-byes. But, probably worn down from two months of previous chemo, my beddy-byes were no bother. Then, geared up on the other 20mg, I was on a chatty high going in for my treatment the following morning. 'Cleaning the house before you came in?' the nurse taking my bloods enquired.

'Yes,' I told her. I'd been up at four thirty, sprucing everything.

'Use it,' she advised. The housekeeping boost was something generally and well appreciated, apparently.

And it won't last, she might have added. The first part of Taxol treatment was an intravenous bag of Piriton, an antihistamine, the side-effect of which is sleepiness, I discovered, as soon as it started dripping into the vein. I pinged almost instantly from the high to nodding off.

That's one reason it's good to have someone along, where possible, when attending treatment. You're on so much medication in addition to the chemotherapy that you're never quite yourself. It's helpful to have another's eyes and ears. My brother Kevin accompanied me that day. I had great chats with whoever came with me, a very positive memory of the whole chemotherapy process.

Unlike the A/C, Taxol isn't administered by hand: the large bag of clear liquid is delivered by intravenous drip. It takes about three hours, the first time slower, while they gauge how your body is responding. You can go into toxic shock, in which case it's immediately stopped and you're injected with adrenalin. That didn't happen to me.

The received wisdom is that Taxol is much better tolerated than A/C. Certainly the nausea is less. But when the full force hit a few days later it was startling: I was woken at four a.m. by the most terrific pain in my legs, as if my knees, calves and feet were being bashed with a lump hammer. Crying with it, I got up, hobbling around my apartment, rustling up whatever painkillers I could find – the tramadol I'd been prescribed, stray paracetamol, some old Solpadeine. With trembling hands I popped a whatever-I-could-find concoction, desperate to ease the pain. It didn't quite work.

The next day I called the cancer nurse to ask if the pains were normal because, I said, I found them OUTRAGEOUS. She said, 'Yes, that sounds normal.' Which made me laugh – 'outrageous', okey-dokey, it's all good. I had a show that night with The Nualas, at the Mermaid Theatre in Bray, County Wicklow, so I went to my local friendly pharmacist, who did all my prescriptions, and asked, 'Help?' He suggested a one-off combination of paracetamol and ibuprofen with the tramadol – just for the night of the show. I found that pharmacist a great support throughout treatment. He explained each medication I was prescribed, was great with advice about side effects, and reassuring because he had experience of many other people dealing with cancer. Advice to anyone embarking on a course of cancer treatment: make sure, if possible, that your pharmacist is approachable and personable.

I'd also put by some steroids to take prior to going onstage for their magic upper-tastic-ness. Man, if they didn't turn you into a tub I could live on dexamethasone. We Nualas had the most fantastically uncomfortable stage shoes at the time – pointy stilettoes that squashed the bejasus out of the toes because they slid the foot forward from the awkwardly high heel. The numbing effect of the painkillers was a delight in that regard. The combined effect of meds and Dr Theatre made it, if not a breeze, not much bother either – my legs and feet ached, there was an unsexy fug of hot sweatiness, but otherwise, it was just great to be up, out, and onstage working. Laughter is … No, I won't repeat the cliché, just to say, it's true.

Another side effect of Taxol, I noted, was that it made my fingers very sensitive. First time round I was wishing I'd cut my nails shorter before it kicked in because they were too hurty to file. I found myself typing delicately, as if the keyboard were brittle glass, when I worked. There was tiredness, but not the same level of fatigue as on A/C. There was nausea but I had the anti-emetics Emend and Motilium to see to that.

I had a big slump on the third day after the show, probably a downer from the steroids. I recall walking into the city centre, just a couple of blocks, to get something to eat. But the usual ten-minute walk took about an hour as I had to go so slowly. It was a humbling insight into the incapacitated reality of the older people one sees shuffling along. I remember bumping into someone I knew in the supermarket, he going, 'And you look great, wow!' And I guess I did, the big flushed steroid face on me, the definitely-not-wasting-away cut of my body. But I was also propping myself up against the wine shelves. I found the comment, the situation, funny, because my whole body was hurting so much right at that time, as he, charming young gay-boy (one of my favourite types of human), nattered away. Then he squeezed my arm once, twice as he left, which was intensely painful. There's a thing I learned, being a squeezer myself: don't squeeze, pummel, pat or otherwise chummily man-handle people on chemo. It just might be Ouch Central for them.

Next time round, at the hospital, as soon as I told the oncologist about the extent of pain, he prescribed morphine tablets, and thereafter the side-effects weren't such an issue. Walking remained something of a problem: for at least one day after each treatment I could barely hobble about, such was the ache in my feet and legs.

If the getting sick was upsetting, the getting well again brought instant amnesia about being sick. But I got heavier, weaker, was hairless, while the Taxol left me with fiery pins and needles in my fingertips, and legs feeling like wobbly numb stumps.

The penultimate chemo treatment was Wednesday, 12

October. For the first time, when he examined my breast, the oncologist said the tumour was responding really well to the chemo.

That day I met a woman who had stage-four HER2 positive breast cancer. For eight years she'd been attending the oncology ward every three weeks for intravenous Herceptin. She told me that when her breast cancer originally occurred she'd agreed to take part in a trial for the then new drug, but she was in the control group. She was happy to accept that, understanding it was part of the deal in doing the trial, but, she said, if she had been given the drug back then the cancer wouldn't have spread, and she'd have stood a good chance of being cancer-free by now. Instead she was tied to the hospital schedule for the treatment that was keeping her alive. However, she was impressively calm, sanguine and accepting of her situation. Meeting people like her really brought home to me how lucky I was.

An older lady beside me had brought her own sandwich. 'Would you ever smell that? Is that sandwich OK? It said October the sixteenth on the ham, but I don't know,' she said to me. I said I couldn't trust my sense of smell either, but I had a sniff and nodded anyway. Chemo really affects some people's taste buds – it didn't much mine. My sense of smell was more noticeably affected: I kept getting weird pongs everywhere. My kitchen started to smell manky, like the poo of newborn chickens. I'd find myself following the pong, sniffing in cupboards, under the sink, never getting to the root of it. The mysterious shitting chickens were all in the imagination of my chemo-whacked nose – I hoped.

Recorded in my diary that day too: a snatch of overheard hospital conversation that amused me.

'How's your wife?'

'She's gone.'

'And what did she have?'

'Lung cancer that went to the brain.'

'And I bet she never smoked in her life.'

'She did, eighty a day.'

A few days later I had a corporate gig at the Mansion House in Dublin for an audience of 650 business women. After drinks, dinner and networking, the focus of the evening was a catwalk show of business wear. I was the light relief in all of this, my job: to talk amusingly about underwear for twenty minutes, 'My Life in Lingerie', the title of the speech. Such gigs can be stressful: will women on an evening out want to listen, be in the mood for comedy? Will the schedule go haywire, and you'll be on stage late to a sea of inebriation? My way to deal with it: over-prepare. The speech was rewritten fifteen thousand times, then rehearsed and rewritten again a couple of times with Sue 'No-nonsense' Nuala, who gave me additional gags: 'Lingerie is a French word, meaning "underwear, but a lot more expensive".' There were several consultations with the client: I appreciated working for a woman who was as particular as I was about getting it right. Plus the distraction from cancer was welcome: the frivolity of the material, of being a comedienne, was a relief. 'What about basques?' women ask me, and I say to them: 'I'm sorry, any piece of underwear named after a region of Spain famous for its separatist guerrillas – one word: "weird".

161

That's like having a pantie called the Bogside. Or a bust bandana called the Gaza Strip. "It's very small, holds in an awful lot, and doesn't feel right whichever way you look at it."'

The ladies loved it. After I'd left the stage the compère mentioned I had cancer. There was an audible gasp, then more intense applause, which really amused me. I felt like I was being applauded for my disease. Breast cancer, is it? I say, well done. And, of course, later, when I was chatting to the women, many had their own cancer experiences to share, with interesting personal insights and perspectives.

And then, as much as the whole cancer seemed interminable, it being over seemed to come of a sudden. On 26 October, I'd thought I'd be cha-cha-cha-ing into the hospital, singing, 'Hooray, today's the last day!' Instead I walked around the apartment sobbing as I got ready that morning. It felt like mourning a loss. I was utterly empty and bereft as I left at eight thirty. My sister, who accompanied me, asked, 'Don't you feel a weight has lifted now the chemo bit is over?'

Treatment was finished by three o'clock. And, no, I didn't. It had been three months of being pricked with needles – blood samples taken and chemo cannulas being inserted into sore veins. Three months of canisters and bags of toxic liquids, with my name printed on them, being slowly injected or intravenously dripped into my system. Three months of my breasts being manhandled by strangers. Three months of physical vitality slowly eroding, as the main tumour visibly shrank. But also three months of regularly touching base with the nurses and the security of hospital care. I talked to other women about it: they expressed that same, surprising, sense of loss. A reflection of the excellence of hospital we attended, you might say!?

Now things were careering toward the next unknown: mastectomy.

14. Sex

The only thing I was ever taught about adult intimacy came from the sex education nun, Sister Don't, who said, 'If you have sex before marriage you will rot in the fires of Hell for all eternity.' So when I inevitably did I thought, Feck it, in for a penny, in for a pound.

An early stand-up gag

Casually flicking through the promotional magazine of a breast-prosthesis company, I came across an ad for 'Yes'. 'Thanks for restoring my sex life and making my daily existence more bearable,' one happy customer called 'Nottingham' said. What was this? I wondered. 'Leeds' clarified in the next quote: 'After chemotherapy and premature menopause I experienced severe vaginal atrophy for three years.' But Yes had done the trick. It was a 'vaginal moisturiser and intimate lubricant'. Isn't 'Yes' something of a misnomer? I thought. I'd have called it 'Oh, no – on top of everything else I'm desiccating.' I had started having sudden hot sweats at night, waking up, pyjamas drenched – 'hot flashes', as they call them in the States. 'I'm still hot, it just comes in flashes now,' wrote a breast cancer patient, being yahoo-positive about her chemo-induced menopause in an Internet chat room. My hot flashes just left me feeling 'Oh, no, "Yes"?'

Luckily I never needed to go the Yes route. Nothing 'atrophied' except my interest in the nookie department. Bald and in the middle of chemotherapy, sex was so far from my thoughts that I couldn't imagine how anyone, in a similar situation, would be up for it. But apparently they were. 'Still use contraception,' the Cancer Society breast cancer chemotherapy advice booklet mentioned, and presumably ladies weren't just rolling rubbers on their beloveds to amuse themselves on low days.

'My husband was very supportive of me, sexually. I needed to wear my wig to have sex,' a cancer acquaintance told me, erasing any remaining ambiguity on the matter. Negotiating your intimate life was part of the whole cancer-counselling conversation. I guess I'm lucky to be alone, I'd find myself thinking, feeling bloated and ill on chemo. The very thought of sex! The very thought of a man's needy eyes on the pillow beside me, radiating a 'Biologically, I need a ride and technically you owe me for all the "being there" I've been doing' vibe, the very thought of pressing my sore, tubby body, with its cankerous tit, against the penetrative masculinity of a chap with the hots who loved me and, ergo, I had to love him back, with my vagina. Even if treatment had turned my lady-bits to prunes, I was glad I didn't have to find that out for a fact one way or the other. I decided to be robustly happy about my single status. Too much information, maybe, but I didn't even masturbate during the whole thing. I felt utterly asexual.

And after it all, after mastectomy, how would I be feeling? I supposed not the most confident about initiating intimacy with anyone. Imagine a first-time birds-and-bees impetus with someone, and you having to interject with an excruciating 'By the way, there's something I should tell you about my chest.' Or them finding out by appalling accident: 'I say, oh dear, I'm terribly sorry, but your breast seems to have come off.' I couldn't, just could *not*, imagine sharing my half-cleavage with someone I hadn't been long intimate with already.

'What would be your first thought if you were told you had breast cancer?' I asked one friend.

'That I hadn't had enough sex,' she answered, mirroring my feelings at the time that cancer spelled the end of sex. Like me, she was a mid-forties singleton. However, unlike her, my thoughts wouldn't have rested on regret about the actual scoreboard, as it were. I had had a good innings – or 'out and innings', you might say. If I'd thought about it at all, I should perhaps have just regretted that, for all the many lovers I'd had, I'd exhibited little talent for 'love'.

My issue in the sex department wasn't about breadth of experience but depth of intimacy. When I looked back from the position of ill-health, it seemed I'd never believed in someone truly being, as the songs say, 'the wind beneath my wings', 'my first, my last, my everything', my 'Puff the magic dragon'. Instead, I might say I ended up mostly with notches on the bedpost. On the one hand I could intellectualise it: I was just a child of my time, my 'love life' was typical enough of a type of dissolute, disconnected, late-stage, capitalistic first-world media-contaminated attitude to human interaction. I could casually joke that, 'The way I look at men is, you can't live with them, you can't have full penetrative sex without them.' I could see my formerly robust sexual urges as healthy appetite, and the charming tumescent men who happened into my hungry maw as most delicious, nutritious, natural feeds for my needs. But on the other, 'Bless me, Father, for I have sinned': hadn't I been terribly naughty altogether? Or, going back to the first hand, wasn't there something simply honest and sacred in honouring the sensuality of one's given nature, by giving it abundant expression? Or, back to the other, *mea maxima culpa*, hadn't I been an awful ould Jezebel altogether?

And there was me, at one point, thinking I was earmarked to be a saint. I remember, as a nine-year-old, in third class in national school, a local priest, visiting from the missions, called in to say hello to everyone. 'Who is that girl?' he exclaimed. He was looking at me. I told him my name. 'Come up here to me,' he said, and in front of the twenty-five or so other pupils, he hugged me tight to his ample, black-shirted body, and said to our teacher, 'Wouldn't she make a lovely reverend mother altogether?' My chubby face burned bright red under his holy hug. Then he made me sing for him, in front of everyone. I gave him my whole repertoire of one hymn: 'The bells of the Angelus are calling to pray ...' It was hugely embarrassing. Having spent a goodly portion of my school career on crayoning pictures of Jesus and the saints, with their bright yellow haloes, I wondered afterwards, Why did I stand out to him? Did it mean I had a special calling, like, say, St Lucy, who gouged out her own eyes for the love of God and her chastity, or Matt Talbot, venerated for not telling anyone he was wearing a load of chains under his underwear all the time, or … Oh, I had a huge list of acclaimed Catholics from the past in my mind. Was I going to be one, or was I merely nun material? My mother always said she'd wanted to be a nun when she was young. Maybe the vocation had skipped onto me. But I was more interested in being a star. Yet Mary O'Hara was on *The Late Late Show* a lot at the time, and she was a nun, wasn't she? Whatever, I was left with a sense that oh-oh, maybe I did have a 'calling', that God was calling me through Mr Huggy, the mission priest.

When I look back it seems extraordinary – there's no way a visiting priest would bound into a class of nine- and ten-year-olds now, choose one, and speculate on their potential future religious vocation while cuddling them close to their belly. It would seem, to say the very least, pervy.

The notion of being a nun, of sincere religiosity in general, faded as my sense of womanhood grew. But that sense bloomed in a very stop-start stilted manner in the hothouse of a rural Catholic education. I remember our secondary-school science teacher, a jaunty farmer-type, with a fondness for green-toned suits that intensified his red-ruddy complexion, introducing the lesson on human reproduction with a strict proviso: No Sniggering. He then drew a diagram of the female reproductive system on the blackboard, turned to us, and said, with a smirk, 'The heifer's head,' which drew the burst of laughter he evidently sought. Yes, undeniably, the shape of the uterus resembled a skinny cow's face, the Fallopian tubes its horns. But to compare the hallowed interiors of us convent virgins to the mug of a farmyard animal was fantastically crude. There was an odd resonance of 'Amn't I a bit of the Jack the lad?' too, which was grossly inappropriate – thus hilarious. And, ultimately, that means it's still the first thing I think whenever I see such a diagram.

Then, sketching the male version of the organs, he noted that, unlike the female with her monthly rhythm, the male was, 'like the battery, Eveready'. He entreated us to snigger through the class he said we shouldn't snigger in. The summation of the whole human reproductive lesson was: this is one hell of a sniggery business.

As teenagers we were told in school that if we ever ended up in a one-to-one situation with a person of the opposite sex the question to ask was: 'If my mother was here would I be doing this?' That question was to set our personal boundaries of what was permissible. Our instructor was a fiercely moralising bullying thug, a now-deceased priest, one of our teachers. He referred to sex as 'the marriage act'. Around the same time he threatened two pupils with expulsion for holding hands on the school premises. Such overt contact was out of public bounds: if they wanted to meet in their own time, say in an isolated field, maybe that would be OK – if their mammies were hidden in a hedgerow shouting, 'Enough, but no further,' presumably. Oh, the complicated innocence of it.

That same priest could seem gentle: 'Are you all right, Anne? You seem to have lost a lot of weight.' He surprised me with the question, falling into stride alongside me as I walked across the school yard at lunch break. I was fifteen. The weight had fallen off as I'd got taller so there was maybe something of a vulnerable gaunt look about me. 'If there's anything wrong, and you need to talk, I'm here,' he suggested.

I was aghast at the idea. Talking! With him! The instinctive answer was 'No! No, of course not. There's nothing wrong. No way.' Even as a bit of me inside wanted to respond, 'Yes, everything's completely fucked, help.' Anyway, that was that.

Years later, as a wave of clerical sexual abuse allegations and investigations swept Ireland, that man stood accused of serious sexual abuses of a vulnerable minor. He passed away before he faced the charges in court. When a chap I'd been in secondary school with shared the information, that schoolyard exchange came back to me, and I found it chilling. In retrospect: what a warped, seemingly innocent environment.

In perhaps some official acknowledgement that school wasn't solely about teens passing exams to get a good job but also, by default, happened to be a vortex of three hundred plus bodies swirling with adolescent hormones, there was once a go at overt 'sex education'. A female teacher read out a pre-prepared talk, and what I most recall of it is the revelation that boys have wet dreams.

I'd never heard of wet dreams before, though from the absolutely mortified look on the boys' faces, all of them rigid in their seats with embarrassment, it was clear they knew precisely what she was on about. Of the areas she might have touched upon, what a thing to choose. More emphasis on the sniggery side of human sexuality, you might say.

For the ordinary ins and outs of sex, we didn't really need any blunt elucidations. Anyone from a farm, which was most of us, would have already gleaned enough about the birds and the bees from the cows not to need an adult's explanation. Americans were always asking their moms and pops about it on telly, which resulted in a dramatic sit-down chat. In the Irish countryside all you had to do was watch cattle and say nothing.

This was how it went with cows anyhow. A cow stood in a field. Other cows got up on her, like they were going into a leapfrog, then thought better of it. Crucially, the standing cow didn't move. The cow 'was calling'. She was driven into a barn to await the AI man. He arrived with a steel canister in his car boot. The choice had already been made from the bull booklet, which had pictures of each bulky lump of a bull, with details of its progeny's characteristics: things like 'easy calving', 'good milkers', 'lean, when meat'. A cloud of cold steam escaped as he opened the canister, picking out the tube of chosen bull-spunk, setting it up in a huge syringe. Putting on long rubber gloves that went up to the elbow, he went into the byre and shoved his whole left arm up the 'calling' cow's arse. He rooted around, eased in the long injection, and she was in calf. Hopefully. The cow swayed her hindquarters this way and that, mooed a bit, maybe looked about, round-eyed at the mad situation happening at her rump. Technically, it wasn't the same as human sex – but you got the general principle. In, out, female confusion, the man drives off – funnily enough, that was how my 'intimate life' panned out, far in the future.

Come winter, the cows calved. You'd see it all: a big new thing coming out a bloody small hole, a key mystery of life itself. You'd be under no illusions about the reality of what 'giving birth' meant. You saw all the harshness of what life can be in the cow barn. There was pitiful lowing from the cow, her back hunched in obvious agony. Sometimes calving required a lot of pulling, ropes around the legs protruding from the bum, farmer straining, cow in distress. A couple of times I saw the baby animal die hanging out the hindquarters. You'd have seen it struggle for a half-breath, seen the light of life in its new, beautiful eye going out. The sight of the delicate pink muzzle, the long-lashed eyes, the beautiful baby mammal, head covered with steaming womb-slither, hanging dead, brought tears to everyone's eyes. Thankfully, it didn't happen that often.

Living calves would suckle a couple of times then be put on milk replacer. I recall sitting at the head of our favourite cow, White Heady, tethered in her stall, just after she'd given birth. Then she'd licked off the afterbirth, nuzzled her baby till he stood, he'd suckled from her udder. And then he'd been separated off to the calf shed. She'd licked me instead, her long, strong cow-tongue rhythmically lapping, her smelly, burpy-breath saliva soaking my anorak with misplaced postnatal love.

Later, her calf would suckle me or my siblings when we taught it to slurp milk replacer from a bucket by putting our fingers under the surface of the warm liquid, and into its mouth. And it never saw Mommy again, the udder milk that Nature provided for it being requisitioned for cheese and yogurt, butter and cream, a range of products I'd read women saying are directly related to breast cancer. Such are the loop-de-loops of going with and against Nature. Asked, 'Pappy, what are the facts of life?' Pappy might as well begin, 'Fact one, honey bun. Life takes no prisoners. It can be a complete bitch.'

You knew that from just watching, if you came from a farm. You knew it as soon as you could see, and take in what you saw.

The big difference with humans was, of course, the sin thing: the veils and knots and hurdles of wrongdoing that enveloped everything about the natural human body. My mother told me she even had to be 'churched' before she could receive Communion again after giving birth to each of us. As she explained it, it was a little ceremony where she was cleansed of the sin of having gone through that. But how could it be a sin if it was inevitable? If you got pregnant, how else was the baby going to come out? So, it was the getting pregnant that was wrong? But the man wasn't having to be cleansed too: why not? And how could any of it be wrong anyway, when it was the most essential thing to survival? 'Contradictionism' could be Catholicism's second name – I don't know how my mother's generation put up with it. I supposed the most blatant, misogynistic contradiction, that the finest, most revered woman of the whole palaver was a virgin mother, was bombed home as a way to soften the brain for absorbing the rest of the incongruity. These were, of course, ways of thinking I evolved later in life.

Well into my teens, I still absolutely bought into the sin bit about sex. I recall praying that I'd never be tempted to indulge in that momentary madness – the giving-in to the illicit urge to fornicate. To be in Hell for ever for a slip-up of passing pleasure? It was a no-brainer. It was bad, too, because it could lead to that other evil eventuality: going for an abortion in (where else?) England. 'That heathen country across the water,' as the priest I mentioned above bombastically condemned it. Who in their right mind would want to slide down the slippery slope of becoming a fornicator-cum-murderer? They were the images set in my head, of pickled innocence vacuumed from wombs, of tiny feet dissected from wanton bodies.

Graphic posters underlined the arguments of the vociferous pro-life movement of the time. I remember going to a meeting, when I was thirteen, for the 'pro-life' campaign. Held in the local parish school, by local concerned housewives, they showed pictures of post-abortion tissue, or dead babies, as they preferred to refer to it. The facts were shocking: defenceless babies were being killed; it had to be stopped. You could buy a little lapel brooch of two metal-alloy baby feet to wear to show the world on which side you stood. Oh, the naïve passion I felt: 'Yeah, I'm definitely against that.' No sense of the complexity of circumstance around such decisions, no context, just bad ladies and, even worse, doctors murdering. Might as well have been 'Campaign Against Being Mean to Cute Puppies' for all the sophistication in the argument.

But such images became mushed up in the notion of what sex was about: sin, baby murder, being cursed to eternal fire under the behest of a mad man-beast on goat hind legs, with hoofs, and burning black eyes, a throbbing red pitchfork and two gorgeously wild buck horns spewing from his demonically fascinating head.

Every year in secondary school there were 'retreats': we retreated from the normal schedule of classes, and visiting priests would provide a few days of Catholic hothousing. 'Bad thoughts are a mortal sin,' was the dominant theme of the elderly fellow my class was landed with when I was sixteen. This was news! It was well established you wouldn't actually be doing it, but now Hell beckoned if you even dreamed of the possibility.

'Don't forget what I said about bad thoughts,' he said, before he went into the ecclesiastical wardrobe of the confessional. If we got knocked down by a car on the way home, say, and kicked the bucket before a priest could make it to our accident to deliver the Last Rites, if we were unaccountably crushed against the convent wall by a reversing school bus and passed away without the opportunity of whispering, into the ear of a father, 'I had heavy petting in my head. I imagined a boy kneading my bare boobies with his naked hands, and I'm heartily sorry,' we were Hell-rot.

I couldn't give him my version of such thoughts. I gave him the usual I'd been using since seven: I said a bad word and I didn't do what I was told. 'And anything else?' he provoked.

'No,' I disappointed him. The chasm between putting into spoken words the dirty privacy of my bad thoughts, and the possibility of Hell for all time, was one I couldn't cross. Anyway, for all his austere holiness, I sensed he was after titillation.

And then there was a quirky anomaly like this: our Catholic convent sexy-records break time – which I always found funny: when it rained during lunch break, the boys went to the sports hall and kicked around balls, and all the girls had 'records' in another assembly room. There was a record player and a stash of convent LPs. Tracks I recall bopping to on those rain-damp lunch times: 'Voulez-vous Coucher avec Moi', 'Gimme! Gimme! Gimme! (A Man after Midnight)' and 'I Love To Love'. There we were in our bottle green Sister of Charity gym-slips, there was Sister Annmarie doing a self-contained jiggle as she supervised, there the music was, telling stories of raunchy goings-on in the evening, asking about going to bed with someone, using the formal French form of address, indicating you didn't know them well, you dirty thing – Sister Annmarie would have been well aware of that: she was the French teacher. Whatever you wanted a man in the middle of the night for, it wasn't putting up shelves or help with conjugating your French. And some of the girls used to do this popular disco move of the time, a sort of all-round-the-body hip-bang between two people, totally suggestive of crotch-activity. Damp, musty lunch breaks of fornicatory lyrics, horny moves – it was a veritable porno-disco break, if you wanted to think of it that way. Then, *brrrrring brrrring*, the electric bell would go off to signal the end of lunch break, and it was back to terminal moraines, the Flight of the Earls, Pythagoras, Monsieur Thibaud and mortal sin.

As if the messages of teachers and nuns weren't enough, there were the good ol' shreds of parental advice: 'When you kiss, you shouldn't let the boy put his tongue in your mouth. It's very double meaning,' my mother told me. I actually, honestly, couldn't figure what she meant. In the same rare moment of sharing, she added, 'Men don't have the same self-control women have.' What might happen? Would his trousers spontaneously explode, no matter how much 'self-control' anti-embarrassment/mortal-sin energy he put into it? The only way to find out was if a boy asked you outside when you went to a disco.

'Don't go outside if a boy asks you' was one of the only pieces of advice my dad gave me. He needn't have worried: it seemed I wasn't the type to be provoking invitations to 'go outside' at discos – out into the glamorous, exciting possibility of a fella pushing me romantically against the pebble-dashed dance hall wall, in the rain. Pushing his tongue between my lips in that mysterious manner that meant 'kiss' and, somehow, not 'yuck, major germs alert'. And then maybe going so far as to explore the audacious bareness of my formerly untouched breasts, with the flats of his school-biro stained hands, and them a bit strangled by all the effort of getting up there, up and under my sparkly disco jumper and tight second-hand bra from cousins in Manchester. While I did what? I didn't know, I could hardly imagine. I longed to know, longingly wondered when, if ever, it might happen to me.

Anyway, you forgot about all that when, at the disco, everyone was moshing in same-sex gangs to the playlist hits of those days: The Smiths, Wham, AC/DC, Bananarama, Tear Drop Explodes, Joy Division, Echo and the Bunnymen, Madonna, Duran Duran.

Those discos: on the high stage at one end, the DJ spun the discs, between two pillars of flashing coloured lights, which provided 'atmosphere'. The room was a rectangle, plain-painted walls, bare-board floor, a hatch for the purchase of Fanta or Coke – *Saturday Night Fever* it wasn't: it was more like jigging about in a bunker amid the glow of manic traffic lights. But it was charged because it was the only outside-school outlet for contact, and for all the fun you were having with friends, the crucial turn of events was when the first bars of either 'Wonderful Tonight' or 'Careless Whisper' whined through the sound system. And the crowd would part like it was the sea and Moses had shaken his stick at it. Girls to the left, boys to the right: the sexes faced each other across the divide of empty floor. Slow set! Yes, more often than not the lads crossing the floor to hunt down a dance didn't come looking to me. But sometimes there was the offer, and then you'd discover the word 'dance' was just a euphemism for mooching about the floor, the boy holding you so tight you were tripping over his feet like together ye were a four-legged, two-bodied monster, stumbling clumsily about to the strains of Eric Clapton telling his lady she was looking mighty tonight. 'Slow set' dancing meant the boy holding you so close it was like he wanted to climb through your skin, as he jammed his sweaty hands to your back like he was cramming for an exam that pivoted on the question 'How many ribs are contained in the teenage lady?' It was, in a word, a bit intense. One minute you were pogoing to, say, a silly, bouncy song about all your senses being on overtime. The next Meatloaf was yowling, intensely, and grindingly slow, about wanting and needing someone, but definitely not being in the market for loving them – yet making it clear he had riding them on his mind anyways – the dirty thing. While you and a boy clung to each other in the kind of embrace that might have been appropriate if you'd just been told the world was about to end, and you actually knew each other enough to want to share your last few moments mashed together.

But it was good because it was contact: it was experience under the belt; it was something I wasn't getting very often. Until, finally, at the age of seventeen, *Finally*, I danced with a boy I found overwhelmingly attractive. And swathes of poetry, heaps of tear-soaked songs and a Shakespearian penchant for lovelorn self-poisoning made sense. The instant attraction was visual: he was tall, thin, different; the physical was there in the insane intensity of touching him in the slow set. Teenage kicks.

After meeting at discos a couple of times, swaying to The Smiths, Bowie and The Smiths again, dancing those slow sets where I felt his whole body tremble against mine, he asked me outside. Me! Outside! Boy! One of the most tense and exciting occurrences ever. I got my coat and went with him. I just presumed he knew exactly what he was doing because he was The Man. He led, I followed. I'd not been 'outside' with anyone before: what did I know?

My previous imaginings went out the window. For someone like me who seemed to half-daydream my way through life, the fact of this actually happening, and of feeling so intensely present in the moment, was stunning. It was like discovering a new level of being alive. We walked up the street. It was raining, it was winter. He chose a deep doorway. At his behest we stood in from the rain. He lifted my chin to turn my face to his, his lips touched mine, our mouths covered each other's and everything happened naturally, amazingly. We kissed seemingly for ever to the sound of rain quietly splashing and dripping all round. And yet it was too short. After, he held his long open coat around me. The streetlamps reflected rivers of light in the roads, the drip of the rain the soundtrack on the memory. Wow! This is what independent adult life will be like, the quiet beauty of subtle intense connection with a man you feel you could fall in love with, I felt. But, thirty-odd years later, I still think nothing has ever topped the intensity of that sweet long kiss, no intimate scenario has ever surpassed its sheer romance, and the sense that, once I'd got over the hump of such a thing actually occurring, it would occur again, and often, was mistaken.

The last summer I lived in Sligo, 1984, I visited him many Sundays, cycling a short-cut, miles through a vast stretch of isolated bog. The flat brown land splayed out either side of that journey like loneliness, not another soul to be met on that road, as across I'd go to his parents' bungalow. The soundtrack of that time was David Sylvian's just released first solo album, *Brilliant Trees*: songs about nostalgia, intense eye contact, poet's blood, trouble between the flesh and the soul, and doubt. In my recall, I was nostalgic for that time even as I was within its ticking, felt as ineffectual as a shadow in it. To hear that album now is to be back in the awful ache of those teenage weeks. I was leaving for Dublin at the end of the summer, I felt rootless. I wished that the feelings I had for that boy could manifest as something more than mainly protracted listening. Something that could have anchored me, us, as I felt everything I knew was about to dissipate in the trauma of suddenly new circumstance, both in moving away, and in the impending disintegration of the family arrangement I came from. Maybe things would have been different had we been more into Men Without Hats or Bananarama – songs about 'safety dances' or Robert de Niro hanging about, speaking in Italian, rather than David Sylvian harping on about playing his mysterious red guitar.

On the last late-August evening, night was drawing in before I left. His father offered me a lift home. No! I insisted. The thought of that boy seeing where I lived seemed unimaginable. His father insisted otherwise. So the bike went in the boot of the car, the boy and I got in the back seat, his father took my bog road home. Halfway there, I said, 'Really, please, let me off here. I'm OK to get home now.' We were in the middle of Nowhere Bog, on an isolated dark bad road. But something in my voice made him comply with my wish. He took my bike out of the boot, got back in while his son said goodbye to me. Goodbye. Somehow the situation made it no kiss. The intimacy of a kiss couldn't have ameliorated the humiliation I felt at having to insist on such an odd request. But the thought of that boy and where I lived, in juxtaposition, was a horror that left me shaking.

His father turned the car around. Its lights faded into the silent gloom of the night. The dark had well and truly fallen. Alone, as my eyes acclimatised, an incandescent mist floating over the flat, heathery peat became apparent. In the ordinary course of events I'd have found that unnerving, it being suggestive of everything ethereal you've ever heard in an Irish ghost story. But a belly-deep, sickening sense of shame superseded fear. The sky was shades of darkest blue deepening to black. The landscape was near black all round me, embellished with intricate shadows of odd fussy hawthorn or whin. The ghost of the mist lay long and parallel to my journey. I cycled slowly home, no lights, bike tyres on rough road the only sound, with the sharp call of a curlew echoing over the bog dykes, like a banshee in the still night. My mother was incandescent with rage when I arrived back – an expression of her fear that something bad had happened to me. It had.

A few weeks later I left Sligo for Dublin, and the boy left to study in another city. Only a few times in passing did I ever see him again. Whatever attraction there was had by then been neutralised, the promise of whatever it had been having missed its moment. The memory of him, of that exceptional kiss, lasted longer and stronger than the ephemeral flash of first intense teenage attraction.

In terms of love, I thought college in Dublin would be an automatic fireworks of delightful experience. I thought that, I being a solo agent in the flow of possibility, life would suddenly (unaccountably) be like the movies. Not one in particular, a mishmash. Perhaps everyone in flared jeans and long scarves on anti-stuff protests; and later round a camp fire on a beach at night (that looked suspiciously like California yet was Dublin). There'd be a selection of politically proactive yet devastatingly attractive chaps with whom to fall in love. Or guys might be in drainpipe trousers, slim jackets and skinny ties, take you to gigs and smoky pubs on mopeds; you'd get lost in the music, beer and love, and you'd have intimate fumblings in bedsits carpeted with swirly designs, papered with *passé* patterns. Or would everybody dress in corduroy jackets with leather elbow patches, and would you fall into infatuation in a fug of old book dust in wood-panelled libraries, while you mutually stuffed your heads with knowledge, and later each other's bodies with the appendages of love, and later, later you went protest marching because being involved in serious issues added significant frisson?

None of it was as above, except the protesting, which didn't even live up to the imagined intensity – 'Who says freeze the fees?'

'Jack Frost!'

'What does Jack Frost say?'

'Freeze the fees.'

That was the call and response when a horde from our college marched with the united hordes from other Irish third-level institutions, protesting against a proposed rise in college fees. The issue didn't even affect me. And it wasn't exactly anti-Vietnam Ville.

Julian Lennon's 'Too Late for Goodbyes' seemed to be the song the radio alarm set off every morning those first few months of college in 1984. Meanwhile Cyndi Lauper was pointing out, in the charts, that 'Girls Just Want To Have Fun'. Indeed! While the Eurythmics countered with news of rain, and Prince added that it was purple.

As for romance, I was with Howard Jones: 'What Is Love?'. As for the chaps in my college class, Tina Turner nailed it: 'What's Love Got To Do With It?' I was literally what Madonna had the sensation of being: 'Like a Virgin'. What to do? 'Jump', according to Van Halen.

Those songs bring back the bad haircuts, smell of hair gel, PLO scarves as fashion accessory, Duran Duran-inspired baggy casual separates of mid-eighties days. And with them the memory of sitting in lectures not daring to engage with the niggling shadow-thought – what am I doing here, actually?

What set in as part of my self-identity at that time was the sense of something I thought I could leave behind in Sligo – unease; things quietly, deeply wrong; inability to take life by the lugs and shake it into a shape that accommodated the person I could be. I'd thought that when I escaped to Dublin it would all be so different. I never imagined it would be so hard. Perhaps most were feeling the same, I don't know, but I felt isolated in the bleakness of not measuring up to myself. And exposed, awkward, it took a surprising amount of 'front' to just walk onto that campus every day. There was nowhere to hide, which was mostly what I longed to do. If I could have completed the degree in bed, alone, under a duvet, I would have. I supposed I might say I didn't have a clue how to actually *live* – proactively, assuredly, with emotional intelligence. But did any of my contemporaries?

So, to sex: looking back over the uneasy landscape of the past from the celibate position of being in treatment for breast cancer and its aftermath, I seem mostly to have operated from my head instead of my heart: I thought of this when the cancer emerged over my heart. As if my body was going, 'Hello, this is what you get for not remembering me', as if the roots of my unbelievable illness were in a wrong attitude – an invitation that was at odds with the clinical, mechanical, digitised, microscopic manner in which the disease was identified and described, in the articulation of treatment paths and delivery of same. At odds with the feeling you could barely name: we're talking about my intimate body, my sexual being – and the heart, my heart. It's over the heart. Is this an accident? The metaphor, honestly, felt as important as the scientific literal.

All my life I seemed to have lived in a half-dream when it came to men, either imagining that through an interlude of sex conjoined deep peace would come, or just settling for the peaks and troughs of delightful but ultimately, post-coitally, lonely not-connecting love and nothing beyond. *Mé féin*, floating off like a bog mist, a banshee, a ghost half manifest when it got to the nuts and bolts of further couple negotiation. I was a combination of sexually promiscuous and relationally celibate.

The complexity, the difference, of another person always scared me: the depth of the other is so unknowable, so fraught with potentially devastating revelation – who knows what odd, ancient fishiness they harbour, deep down? Too risky to go into it: a charmer on the outside but in his heart the Loch Ness Monster. Every chap was potentially that, and more than a few of them crossed my path.

To mangle the maritime metaphor, most of my men became that cliché, ships passing in the night – some fantastic yachts, some has-been canoes, some masquerading as the former, but turning out to be the latter, and vice versa. That was what it was all about. At the very least it was a basis for stand-up material, obfuscatory, tenuously true, the real truth compromised in the dig for the comic:

Ever wake up in the morning, see the head of a man on the pillow beside you, you don't remember going to bed with him? And the first feeling you have is guilt? It shouldn't be. The only time you should feel guilty is if you wake up in the morning, you go down to the kitchen, and when you open the fridge to get the milk you see the man's head in there. And you think to yourself, Flip it, I forgot to get milk again.

Ever wake up in the morning, stretch out your arms thinking, That was a great night last night, I can't remember a thing. And your hand touches something. A man you don't remember going to bed with. And you decide to sneak out before he wakes. You slip from under the duvet, grab your clothes, dress quickly, in the hall, click the front door quietly behind you, and then just RUN away. And you know in your heart and soul it's such a stupid thing to do, particularly if you went back to your place.

Ever have a one-night stand with a guy and find yourself thinking, I wish there were some rules, some etiquette, bed-tiquette, around this. Like recently when a guy said to me, 'What would you like?' Now, to me, we didn't know each other well enough for him to ask such an intimate question. OK, we were naked in bed together. And we'd been through foreplay: we'd been drinking all evening together, but still. I didn't know what to say. So he repeats, 'Seriously, Anne, what would you like?' And I was so delighted he remembered my name, I said, 'Well, if you really want to know … What I'd like is if this one-night stand would turn into a relationship. I'd love if we could get married within the year, get a nice little house by the sea, have a couple of kids, fairly soon, I'm not getting any younger. And I'd like to never allow the kids become drudgery as I've seen happen to other couples, but for us to acknowledge them as the unique expression of our love that they would be. And then when they eventually fly the nest, we two could grow old happy and content together.'

And there was a silence, and he said, 'Would it be OK if I just stuck my finger up your arse instead?' And I said, 'OK.'

A joke I particularly recall sharing with an audience of elderly ladies, in the Town Hall Theatre in Galway, because I thought, despite the robustness of the final line, they'd appreciate the sentiment, a classic collision of male and female desire, a reflection of the complexity of sexual politics in a permissive era. WRONG! The gasp that went through the room, the sudden atmosphere change, was as if a bomb had gone off and sucked the air out. No point pleading, 'But I was trying to say something TRUE.'

I was trying to evoke something of the sense of deluded romance that I harboured through a litany of modern non-committal sex situations. I once recorded this in a loose poem that I'm under no illusion is 'good poetry' but that I like nonetheless for all the banal detail that seems to have left more of an impression than the very man himself. To whom I cannot put a face or name.

I ate the hot sausage off your piece of pizza
When you were just a stranger in the kitchen
Watching the oven
And I was a gate crasher raiding the fridge
Mixing cold Bud and hot punch
While the helium balloon tied to my pinky
Bounced off the cabinets

I've Got Cancer, What's Your Excuse?

And stroked your ear.
Your smile was a closed-lipped curve
I laughed
You laughed too
And looked into my eyes
And I looked back into you.
We were dancing to a hit
When I tripped over an accountant
And you fell on my lips.
Outside there were stars
We staggered
To balance
Our bodies
Then cold
We went to get our coats and go.
Someone skinning up
Offered us a toke
A cloudy edge to drunkenness.
I watched smoke threads unwind from your lips
And thought, All of this moves in a straight line,
The ABC of us.
At your place
Off your face
You found your key, the door, the lock,
You remembered where your bedroom was.
The earth didn't move,
Time didn't stop.
You never phoned.
Neither did I.

As I got older, I tried to be the sensible modern woman, proactive about meeting The One. The Internet! I tried that! I put up a profile saying specifically I'd like to meet someone 'in or near Dublin'. Cue the email from the guy in the San Fernando Valley, suggesting we meet for a coffee at the weekend. Could I be bothered informing him, 'Hey, Bud, I'm from Old Europe, other side of substantial ocean, i.e., NOT NEAR.' Answer: no. Then there was the guy on the horse, in the Australian outback, and the Tokyo businessman beaming beside his Ferrari, and the Italian preening near nude on a beach. And then the Irish guys I actually met, who never added up to the promise of their profiles, which had as much to do with my powers of projection as their inability accurately to assess things like how tall they actually were. The Irish comedienne Alison McKay said she saw that a guy on the Internet had written, 'Hey, ladies, don't lie about your age, we can tell.' She replied to him, 'Hey, guys, don't lie about your height, we can tell.' The height was such an issue with Irish guys that when I actually did meet a guy who was a genuine six foot four, we became 'involved' for several years – the length of time it took me to realise that generous verticality alone does not a 'relationship' make.

I tried singles ads in newspapers: I got in touch with a guy who described himself as enjoying 'writing and reading'. We talked about the journals he kept. 'And what was the last book you read?' I asked.

'I don't really read books,' he said.

'But you mentioned reading in your profile?' I queried.

'I read what I write,' he said. Admirable self-sufficiency, you might say, if you were desperate.

'I've heard there's a singles club in the Conrad Hotel every Wednesday. We should check that out,' a single friend suggested.

I did.

'Oh, yeah, the Minus One Club,' said the receptionist who answered the phone. 'I don't know what happened to that.'

'Obviously it worked: they're all one up by this stage,' I said. I Googled 'Minus One Club' and this came up: 'Amputee Shoe Swap – having one leg and buying a pair of shoes is just a bit ridiculous.'

And then from minus one to multiples: I found myself, at a certain stage, going a bit bananas about the whole game – well, that's my excuse. Driven perhaps by Nature's weird ways in my final flourish of fecundity, a couple of years before cancer, I found myself thinking I must attend an orgy before it was too late, before I was too old. Or dead. I'd always been fascinated by what it must feel like to be in the anonymous abandon of multiple nude limbs, the eroticism of multiple aroused bodies *in flagrante.*

Recently I found myself explaining it to a friend thus: the atmosphere of open eroticism was very freeing, and the sublimation into purely physical communal pleasure massively positive and, er, rather banally, relaxing. 'Dionysian abandon', I might call it in an effort to give the experience a veneer of historical, ancient Greek, ancient human context and respectability. But given everything

I am culturally, given that I cannot say I would happily have my mother there witnessing the activity, such an experience carries a taint of transgression that makes it a thoroughly unrespectable thing I engaged in. A very naughty thing altogether. A Dutch or German person might go, 'It was just human experience you went for, big deal.' Through the lens of, say, the French-style TV programme *Eurotrash* it was an out-and-out nudie comedy sketch. It was probably my old friend the deeply ingrained Catholic guilt that gave it such a mind-blowing edge.

As I write, I recall one Mass when I was a child: the parish priest was telling the story of the woman who spent her whole life looking for the perfect man. But when she finally found him he wasn't interested because he was looking for the perfect woman. What was his point? Marry Quasimodo now if he asks because George Clooney mightn't be interested later on?

The thing was, through all my assignations and effort, ultimately I just could not visualise settling down with a man. Perhaps, having come from a strained family situation, I was intimidated by the notion of having to fit in with someone else's family. That I'd have to explain to the judgemental committee of some potential life-partner's kinfolk the situation I came from.

I was, looking back, still carrying the ancient shame of where I was raised, trailing the baggage of the past I had sought so much to escape. I mention that to my siblings, and they cannot relate to the level of unease and negative self-consciousness I experienced. Older now, and in the throes of cancer, it was really hard to see what had mattered so much; everyone has their issues. And even potential partner's-family problems are easy to see off at the pass: avoid any man who mentions the words 'my mammy' on a first date; ditto he who mentions 'I am royalty/from a billionaire dynasty/fifth generation Cosa Nostra/forty-nine, but I still live with my mammy' – which loops back to the original. See? Not that hard.

Perhaps, though, my primary issue with men may be articulated as something else, not entirely unrelated: I just didn't know what I ought to want or expect from a man beyond sex. I operated on the premise: I want sex, he wants sex, I love sex, win-win. Then I'd be thinking, Hang on, aren't I supposed to want something more? Aren't I supposed to make him realise that he wants it too? Isn't that the freaking dynamic that makes the world go round? But: I didn't know how to play that game, as if there was one.

I know women who would say, 'It's all a game.' Who would say, 'You have to be the proactive one in bagging a chap.' And what you must do, apparently, is use reverse psychology: you're after him but you have to make him feel it's the other way round. You must create a classic 'chase him until you let him catch you' scenario. But how? By following 'rules'. If you don't have an intuitive sense of them (I didn't, evidently), you can purchase tons of books on the topic. They cover every possible angle, from what to wear on a first date to how to spot if he's linked to the al-Qaeda network to when to allow him first see your bottom in natural light. (Tip: he probably won't be interested in your naked bottom if he's linked to al-Qaeda.)

In this version of events it's the woman's responsibility to be in control. In a relationship she must be vigilant and proactive, asking questions such as: 'Where are we going?' 'What are we doing?' 'What do I want from this?' Was I ever asking myself such questions? Yes, but apparently answers such as 'To Kinsale for the weekend', 'Having a bit of craic', and 'I don't know' are just not good enough in the long run.

So, come cancer time, I was a singleton. I recalled a woman, K, who lived all alone up an isolated old road near where we grew up in Sligo. Her transport was an ancient bike, her coat was tied with string, her feet ever in raddled wellies. A ladder and all sorts were stacked in her kitchen, I saw once when I looked into her house. My mother said she'd been belle of the ball once upon a time, could have had anyone, even the bank manager in the town, or a glamorous visiting Yank, according to legend, but the father wouldn't let her go – she'd eventually ended up alone: a 'spinster', a term that didn't sound as much craic as a bachelor. You certainly couldn't imagine a brand of tinned food called 'Spinsters'. How lonely her life must be, I used to think. The thought of such isolation scared me when I was young. I never wanted to be alone. And, cue music from *Tales of the Unexpected*, perhaps that childhood fear was a premonition of adult inevitability. At least, as a rural colloquialism expressed it, I wouldn't, like many Irish Good Catholic unmarrieds gone before, 'die wondering'. But what had all my 'at least I won't die wondering' adventuring been about?

A lover once explained that he considered sexual passion like a rocket that propels the spacecraft of the relationship spaceward. Thus launched, it can fulfil its true goal, the serene orbit of successful coupledom. He was my ex by then, and had succeeded in the rocket launch with somebody else. While half-a-lifetime of my sexual passion seems to have instantaneously dissipated into the ether.

I recalled the comment of the guy who said I had nipples you could hang wet duffle coats on. He was someone I'd have entirely forgotten, other than that piece of Irishman poetry he expressed. It was more evocative than merely observing, say, that he thought I had large nipples. But not quite erotic because it left me with the image of two sopping, unstylish coats hanging off my lovely bust. Yet it was that comment I recalled when I read:

Breast tissue: Left. Specimen size: 220 x 200 x 30mm. Specimen weight: 0.872kg. With attached skin: Yes. Skin dimensions: Medial to lateral 190mm, superior to inferior 90mm. Inked black at deep surface. Sliced at 5mm intervals from medial to lateral into 12 slices. A1-A7 random sections through upper inner quadrant … A20-A21 sections through nipple.

An extract from the lab report post-mastectomy. You don't get given it, I went looking for it. I had to read stuff, as well as being told things, as well as seeing the results of the operation, the clinical description in such sharp contrast to what that organ had meant to me. All its intimate sensual pleasures, its softness, whiteness, erotic mass, all the antithesis of how it ended its days, dissected and sliced dead flesh in an anonymous lab.

The report description 'A20-A21 sections through nipple' in particular, felt like a knife going into me, each time I read it – and I read it over and over, to try and lessen the hurt of it, to absorb the bald fact of what had happened.

Who sliced my dead breast, I wondered, and did they think beyond it being a tagged tissue specimen to what it had been before? An organ that had bloomed on a girl telling her she was a woman. That had made her happy because it was half of a fine pair. That had been a point of joyous, erotic contact in half her sexual lifetime's most intimate situations.

Much as I told myself, 'Don't milk this, it's no big deal,' I could feel it was. And one thing that stuck was a regret that no one intimate with its formerly warm flesh would mourn its absence too. No man who had ever known it knew the loss; no man would hold a hand softly to the wound where once that erotic most-sensitive body part had been, and say, 'It doesn't affect the way I love you because we've long gone deeper beyond that.' It left an emptiness, considering all that shared and shed intimacy; it felt like something had been wasted, had been lost.

15. Death

NUALA: We come from the country, from a very
small place – The kind of place, the suicide rate is
very high.
NUALA: There were six of us when we started out.

The Nualas Trio, 2001

N obody wants to be regarded as a depressive. Isn't
this the positive-fantastic way life is supposed
to be in our current scheme of things? You get
a career with escalating pay, promotion and satisfaction;
your body is your temple, buffed to its best through
exercise and diet, making it fit for a wide range of available
pursuits from windsurfing to recreational tango, your
choice, plus sex in a multitude of exciting and orgasmic
positions, in the context ultimately of a monogamous
relationship that produces two progeny, a boy, a girl; you
end up with a mortgage, a four-door saloon, insurance,
pension and a satisfying sense of being just like everyone

else, tempered by your unique individuality as expressed by the breakfast cereal you prefer and the interior colour scheme of your family property.

As opposed to life as I've experienced a big chunk of it: you just want to sleep as much as possible. I'm one of the many of us who get depressed.

I've thought I could cure it by paying a professional listener to help me trawl through a debris of childhood memory to rebuild a better foundation of 'outlook on the world'; or by reading the right books to re-programme my thoughts into a consistent pattern that might better enable me to function in the world; or by adhering to a spiritual view of the world, the core tenets of which, discipline and acceptance, would calm the unending unease. Or, more dramatically, by naming it an 'illness' and arming myself with meds, ending it; or, most dramatically, a choice many choose, but not me, evidently, by naming it the 'winner', giving up the fight, ending it by ending all – though I have fiddled with that thought endlessly, and found comfort in the possibility of it.

Depression has been the bane of my life. I've seen it variously as a failing, an illness, a cross to bear, an embarrassment. It's not something you want to admit to. Busy and up with life, that's what we're meant to be. What did I do today, I'm asked, and, like a yummy mum in some TV advert, I'd love to be saying, 'Well, I bounced out of bed, showered with sexy soap, almost wanted to ride my armpits they looked so horny in the mirror as I deodorised, Shake n' Vac'ed the pad, skipped to work, did Zumba for lunch, picked up the two kids in the four-door saloon, painted the porch Bongo Pink, booked a family windsurfing/tango holiday, bought some new insurance (in the process almost wanted to ride the household modem, the new broadband is so fast), and rounded off my whole optimally packed day by satisfying my spouse with a Jamie Oliver casserole.'

Rather than my 'day', as it often was: I had a cup of tea and nearly brushed my teeth. It seems like we're allowed to love others or a puppy or a type of chocolate but not ourselves enough to address when we're sick with feelings, nothing more than feelings. You're a drip, self-indulgent, self-obsessed, a loony: all these stigmas hang over admitting to depression.

It's an illness you can't easily admit to, like diabetes or cancer. It's not about some obvious physical misfiring in bodily function; it's about obscure dysfunction in the complicated windmills of your mind. Or is it dysfunction, when the family you were raised in, the society you operate within, the stresses and strains you find placed upon you, may be dysfunctional? Ah, the imprecise science of psychological probs: how to diagnose, how to treat, when the naming of the disease and proffered cures inexorably come from within the very system that's part of the problem. The structure of modern society! Life! The human condition itself!

'Trouble with the nerves,' they used to call it when I was growing up. 'She has trouble with her nerves,' you'd hear said of someone, and if she'd sought GP help back then it would probably have been an ongoing prescription of Valium to anaesthetise the pain of being alive. Did they ask, back then, 'Is it situational or dispositional?' And even if that were delineated, the process of addressing precisely what to do was more complicated than the parameters of an average GP visit could address.

Until my mid-thirties I'd never considered accessing conventional medicine to deal with the Big D. Without really thinking the attitude through, I had an automatic, received idea that the medical approach to mind problems was on a spectrum that went from sedation with prescription pills at one end to ECT, padded cells and lobotomies on the other. You could be sectioned – who hadn't heard the threat 'I'll get you put away' used in Ireland, to get the wife or a wild daughter or an unwanted unmarried sister out of the way, for reasons of shame, hate, control over land or assets or any of the negotiations of power that go on between people? It was said people had been locked away in Irish asylums their whole lives, nothing wrong with them at all other than at some point in their unfortunate existence they'd crossed somebody close to them. A lot of latent negativity pertained to the notion of letting anyone official know you had difficulties in the head department, of getting involved with that potentially devastating powerful system.

But after half a lifetime of fighting recurrent and worsening bouts of utter bleakness, finally, I did talk to my GP about it. And on her good advice, I gave counselling a go. It was straightforward, open-ended, talk therapy: you talk and cry, they listen and hand out the hankies. I struggled to ignore my automatic inner niggling voice's commentary: 'Oh, and would you listen to her, bellyaching about herself. It's far from people who go on and on with the me-me-me that you were reared. What do you think you are at all? American? Give over!' That was the first thing to overcome: the embarrassment about being there at all, talking. The fear you were just spewing a load of boring old rubbish, compounded by the counsellor's intense listening, sucking it all up like their ears were little Dysons, either side of their head.

I stopped and started the process over several years, with several different therapists, talked through the past, felt old hurts and tried to resolve them in the retelling, found ways of naming the feelings around them, came to know myself and my history better by putting a clearer narrative spin on 'what happened'. But maybe it was my innate impatience with a process that, by its very nature, takes time. Or maybe that I couldn't get over the ingrained inner niggling resistance, or believe that you could just talk yourself into feeling, *Yes*, life is absolutely worth living. Whatever, ultimately, I felt, it hadn't worked, it cannot work. Depression, one; talking, nil. I gave up on it. I couldn't afford it any more, anyway. It can cost an arm and a leg to address your head. It didn't help being recurrently riddled with insecurity and doubt about money. Having pitched my lot in terms of creative goals, as I hit my mid-thirties I lost a grip on what those goals were. I wondered should I, could I do something completely different? And, if so, what? I'd get catatonic with fear about being penniless. I regularly recalled something my father repeated throughout our childhood, that we, my brother, sister and I, were nothing but financial liabilities. Now I felt as if I was too, to myself, I felt like a failure, incapacitated by anxiety, fearful I didn't have the ability to keep going enough not to go under. And that deeply ingrained old sense of being nothing if you weren't 'financially viable' killed me. I felt increasingly worthless. If I had someone, The One, could he have helped, been a duvet, a bed, a rock, a solace in all this? Or would he have been repelled by the vulnerability, seen it, me, as a liability? I needed to change utterly, be totally different, right the utter wrong of me. But I couldn't.

Eventually I went back to my GP, expressing again that I couldn't manage with the way I was feeling. Again the floodgates opened as I put words to it, and felt, again, the relief of sharing that inner ongoing negative pressure. This time she suggested something I'd always resisted: medication. On the one hand I'd read plenty about how imprecise a science head meds are, the manipulation of trial results by powerful pharmaceutical companies, the distorting lucrative economics involved, the uncertainties about what the various chemicals do precisely, and long-term, to that most magnificent and complex structure in all of creation: the human brain. On the other, I was desperate. I tried Lexapro, an SSRI (selective serotonin reuptake inhibitor), aimed at increasing the availability of the 'feel good' neurotransmitter serotonin in the brain. And then Effexor, an SNRI (serotonin-noradrenaline reuptake inhibitor), which does similar, but also works on the neurotransmitter noradrenaline (also known as norepinephrine). I stayed on the latter for two years, felt it was helping. Although people close to me said that they experienced me as 'un-centred', it bumped me out of the morass, and after the two years I told my GP I felt ready to come off it. I was OK for a few months, but gradually slipped back to where I had been. I wondered was it the case that, though head meds might lift you out of the abyss, you risked slipping to depths much deeper if you dared to come off them. At that time, the writer David Foster Wallace ended his life, and when I read about his lifelong struggles with depression, it seemed as if that had been part of the picture for him.

The place I entered when it turned dark was darker than ever it had been. All I wanted, absolutely, then, was to die. Die, death, end, kill yourself, exit, good night – variations on such thoughts spun constantly round my head. By then I was in my early forties and everything felt like 'The End'. I'd experienced much and felt there wasn't more I wanted to experience. I'd expressed a lot creatively, and felt that that well was empty. I was virtually post-reproductive, and was dealing with the meaning of being a single non-fecund woman in our sexualised society, getting used to being, if not 'older woman', then definitely 'not young woman'. Being youthful and OK-looking had been a currency that had bought me casual attention and little daily breaks, which, until they disappeared with the onset of evident ageing, I'd never really paid heed to. It was as if, unaware of it happening, I had slipped out of fashion.

Even if I could claim not to be overly concerned with the physical presence I projected in the world, the new casual ignoring was hard not to notice. Furthermore, even if, as girlfriends admonished, I was still attractive, and partnership-viable, depression made me feel utterly asexual. And as always, when I was down, I gained weight, compounding the personal negativity. I was super-sad, kind of fat, no craic, not sexy, and my head played the idea of dying over and over again. These weren't the kind of tantalising personal attributes you'd lash down in a romantic small ad to reel in Mr Right. Unless your ideal date was the chap with the scythe, the black cloak and the face that launched a thousand Hallowe'en masks.

Since I was a kid I'd grown into the habit of thinking of self-death as one of life's options. It seemed a logical background notion. What was different when I hit rock bottom the year or so before cancer was that such thoughts came to dominate, and were constant. There is such shame in feeling this way, to want nothing more than nothing. It rests uneasily alongside the more dominant motif of positive personal responsibility: the narrative that says your thoughts create your feelings; imagine the best you can be, and be that optimal person – it's all here, you are the architect of your own destiny; you can be, and have, everything. And if you don't and haven't, it's your own fault. When you're depressed, this type of self-help philosophy only serves to enhance your sense of alienation, the deep sense of personal failure when you can't be UP WITH PEOPLE.

When I'd been on Effexor I'd written a newspaper column about coping with depression from the perspective that I was on top of the problem. And Jim, a chap involved in suicide prevention, had written to inform me of the four stages of the suicidal process. It starts with thoughts of ending one's life; then 'intent'; 'planning' and, finally, making an 'attempt'. He asked that I alert readers to the importance of getting help right at the beginning of this trajectory, to take it seriously. It's so easy to pooh-pooh such thoughts as mere mental weakness. But when I slipped back, I didn't take his message on board because, having been through counselling and on medication, I felt I'd already explored the 'getting help' options. And they hadn't worked for me. So I'd given up.

I'd got to the point of planning how I would do it. One evening, I went home, having been at an exhibition opening, with the absolute intention that I would go ahead. Self-evidently I didn't, or, cue the *Tales of the Unexpected* theme again, I'm ghost-writing my own book. But that night I came as close as I have ever been to following through. What stopped me were thoughts of what it would do to the people I loved.

It came down to that single crystal-clear thought: I loved them more than I hated my life. I could not leave the hurt and loss that taking my life would cause. It was a legacy I couldn't take upon myself to leave.

I had seen the reality of what it would mean. There had been two occasions when my little sister hadn't been able to get in touch with me and, knowing my state of mind, she had hunted me down and ended up sobbing, saying, 'I thought you were gone.' Enough hurt to others.

I'd heard that reality very early in my life, one morning when I was ten or eleven. A neighbour came knocking at the door, calling out for there to please be somebody there, please. I heard my mother answer, and bring her in and, in a place where everyone was always so circumspect, the gut-distress that unstoppably flowed in her utterances was shocking to my earwigging ear. It was a wailing of something unbearable having happened. It was, I later discovered, the sound of a mother having just found her late-teens son hanging dead, the noose he'd made to take his own life round his neck.

He hadn't come home that night so she'd gone looking for him early, first to a nearby derelict cottage that had been a sort of 'den' for him. She'd found him within, dead. A detail I recall hearing, that she'd seen his feet first, hanging above the floor, visible through the broken bottom of the front door. And then she'd gone running, running up and around the roads, a hefty middle-aged woman running blindly in a place where you never saw middle-aged women running. Until she came to the first house, ours, and my mother let her in. That was all she could articulate. 'Why did he do it why did he do it why did he do it?'

Over and over she wailed the same words. Like he'd ended her life, too, when he'd chosen to end his own, she having lost one so close, meaningful and beloved to her.

The finality of death is mind-blowing, when you're faced with it, the loss beyond loss, the absoluteness. Kevin, Una and I are so close. 'We've borne witness for each other,' as my brother once put it to me. I wouldn't be the one to break the trio of us. I wouldn't be the one to upset the balance of mutual support with dear friends by instigating the explosive full stop of my own death.

But that's the awful thing about the deep end of depression – it's so selfish. When I'd come close to the point of grasping what seemed the only solution, I was absolutely resolved it would be final, and not as anything that could be deemed a 'cry for help'. I had researched how to make it so. I would not want to live as someone who had tried to die. I knew a woman, my age and in a similar career, for whom that had been the case, knew that her first attempt had been her pact with death. Knew, when she was then in the care of a 'mental institution', in the company of people who were at entirely other points of 'insanity', medicated but intelligent enough to know she had already entered the realm of 'the end', she was going to go there whatever. She bided her time. Twice she 'fooled' her carers into giving her release, twice she attempted suicide again, and on the second attempt succeeded by doing it in an extreme manner. I could empathise: it seemed to me she felt already dead from her first attempt. By then she'd lost her job, her apartment; she was in debt from paying for expensive therapy that she had hoped would help. She faced starting again from less than zero whenever she was finally released from institutional care, deemed cured enough to continue – what? Released back into almost insurmountable struggle, with no job, no income, no home, and the stigma of all she'd been through to carry – these were the enormous issues on her horizon.

I attended her funeral on a bright spring day during my own bleakest time. The church was behind a school, the children screaming and laughing in the manic activity of a play break as I walked up to the chapel, the birds chirping in the budding trees, the sun breaking through a sky of white-patched cloud in sudden stunning snatches – everything redolent of Life. Her coffin was being removed from the hearse for her funeral Mass as I arrived. I knew she had made the right decision for herself. There could be no help once you had gone there. Now or never. I had reached that point. And dithered. Perhaps it was that I hadn't slipped those extra notches of losing all income and home, that I had those basic life requirements still in place and, as I have said, the love of my beloveds still shimmered even in the blindness of the dark. I had reached that edge, withdrawn, felt subsequently that that moment had been a now or never.

Yet I still struggled. Things seemed to stutter to a stop. I have the image from that time of sitting by the sea at Dún Laoghaire, south Dublin, the water undulating, sparkling sapphire under the high sun, a light breeze, a perfect day. And nothing in the beauty before my eyes, or any meagre potential my mind could muster – a fuck, a film, a glass of wine – could cut through the numbness. I was crumpled and crying on a bench. It felt like I was vomiting tears, like the last of me wanted to drain out in eye-wet, yet the conscious emptiness was left with its useless arse on cold stone, sick of it, of everything. Then a rat ran out along the walkway. How apt, I thought, the skulking ugly running under everything. Poor rats, they get such bad press.

Then a man I didn't see until he was right beside me asked, 'Are you all right? Is there anything I can do?'

'No, no,' I insisted, startled at the sudden unwanted

presence. I was, I saw myself through his eyes, a woman howling in distress. Clutching myself, rocking back and forward. How embarrassing – fuck it.

He walked on, and came back. 'Are you sure there's nothing I can do?'

No. I shook my head. Definitely no. What could be done, at all, or by him, a chap in a tatty jacket, wheeling a raggedy racer, a geezer taking his bike for a walk along the sea front? Take me up on the saddle and push me into relief? We either fall in love in that unlikely moment, me being fairy-tale saved, or he would push me off the end of the pier and into death by sea water. They say drowning is a most pleasant way to go, once you give in to it.

I was, at that time, dead already. To be still extant was a technicality, was hell.

'You should phone Ruan,' my sister said, soon after. She was referring to an old friend, who had become a counsellor.

'Yeah,' I said, in a tone that said, 'No, I won't.'

'Gimme your phone,' she said. 'I'll take his number and do it.' She wrote down a number, made a call that, she told me later, went like this. She asked was this Ruan. He, rather distractedly, said yes. She asked did he have time to talk. He said yes, for a moment. She milled into outlining the suicidal stasis I seemed to have slipped into, and she wondered, professionally, what he might consider could be done.

'Well, I don't know Anne that well, and off the top of my head I can't think of anything,' he replied, 'and, erm, actually, I'm about to do a children's party.'

'This is Ruan?' she asked again.

'No this is Ruben.'

'Oh,' Una said.

She'd accidentally rung an old comedy friend of mine, a mime artist.

Given the outrageously personal nature of the information she'd just shared, they both found the mistaken identity hilarious. She hoped I would too when she had to tell me, and sure why wouldn't I? Her concern had been the beautiful thing, and the outcome of her effort was beautiful in its comedy.

When Ruben called a while later to check in after the odd Una call, we laughed long and hard about it, that the wrong number she had called had been to, of all people, a comedian. And I told him one of my brother's favourite stories. The suicidal man who goes to his doctor says he can see no point carrying on, life has lost its lustre and he wants to end it all. And the doctor says, 'Listen, there's a circus in town, and there's a clown in that circus, and he's the finest clown there is. Go see him. I guarantee you'll laugh so much you'll be relieved of your burden.' And the man said, 'I am that clown.' Ba-dum ching.

And I harked back to a good review The Nualas had once got from the *New York Times* in which I had been labelled 'a quick-witted uninhibited clown'.

Later, I called my old counsellor chum Ruan, and he advised checking out a suicide charity. I visited their premises in Lucan, Dublin, for an assessment meeting. The waiting area was a bright conservatory; I was given tea in an elegant cup. There was one other client, a woman across the room. We ignored each other as a radio played: a talk show in which a shrill-voiced woman was reporting live on trying one of those fish-nibbling foot treatments. 'I'm putting my feet in the tank now ... Oh, my God, it tickles.' The chat disintegrated into her screaming with laughter, the male host in the studio responding likewise. The escalating peals screeched through the radio, between me and the other woman, each of us silent in our mutual misery. On and on it went. I loved the anomaly, the ear-bursting hooting between us, two total miserables drinking tea from grand cups.

I was offered six sessions of cognitive behavioural therapy with a counsellor in a clinic they ran. Christ, if you didn't have depression before going through that particular environment, it could have kicked you over the line. The meeting room, pleasant enough, was in a church smack-bang in the sprawl of a run-down old housing estate, on the edge of urban Dublin. Further on, fields swept to mountains. Having that relief of greenery within view only accentuated the dismal concrete poverty of the place. But again, the crockery they used when you got the tea or coffee was always better than you'd expect, as was the quality of the proffered biscuit – these were the kindnesses I recall, the acknowledgement that you might have excessive sensitivity to such things if you were feeling mentally raw. It was a tiny kind way of saying, 'Though you may not feel it right now, you are worth something, at the very least more than a teabag floating in an ould chipped mug.' Shame they couldn't have lagged the whole area in a veneer of that pristine delft. The cups of hot beverage and the kindly woman in neat knitwear, listening and chatting advice for six hourly sessions, didn't chase off the black dog: I lacked the strength to instigate the CBT tricks she suggested. Instead I'd just go home, crawl under the duvet and cry, disgusting myself with my endemic lack of 'get on with it'.

So then I tried 'Tomatis'. A friend insisted I give it a go, claiming it had been transformative for her. Tomatis is a protracted aural-stimulation treatment, involving listening to Mozart violin concertos, Gregorian chant and electronic buzzing through 'special headphones'. It left me a bit bemused, and broke. The philosophy of the treatment, in the context of depression, was that aural stimulation is fundamental to mental health. The ear is the first sensory organ to develop in the womb and, goes this theory, depression can be physically characterised as a loss of ability to hear higher frequencies. The preliminary tests proved I had compromised ability in that area, which improved over the course of treatment. It cost thousands of euro, which constituted the last of my spare cash, and then some, but I was desperate at the time. I can't say it 'cured' me, but taking the time out to do it was healthy, just in terms of admitting there was something profoundly 'wrong'.

One day during my treatment, a television producer called with an interesting offer – I kept my phone on, beside the Tomatis couch, in case a work call came through. It's the Murphy's Law of the freelance: as soon as you say you're 'taking a break', the good job offer comes in. He asked if The Nualas would re-form to do an hour-long prime-time television special for RTÉ. It was a request more heartening than ten years of Mozart and the buzz of Tomatis could ever have been for me. An excuse to ask my old work colleague, Sue, again, 'Don't you think it would be worth re-forming The Nualas this time?' We'd been ten years off the road. I'd long wanted to re-form the group, and suspected this was the impetus Sue would go with. The offer was exciting for that reason in itself, not the possibility of a good hour of telly time. The nitty-gritty of it was that the producer was including us in an open-call pitch. Much former experience of developing or being part of proposals for television had proved that 999,999 times out of a million, despite the best creative effort and intentions, the telly thing doesn't happen in the end – as indeed happened again. But a better thing had: the group was re-formed.

Yet, back to the black mutt, even as we were back onstage, achieving an instantaneous standing ovation at our relaunch gig in Dublin's Vicar Street venue, doing prime-time radio and telly shows, I was flat. It was as if I'd walked with the constant thought of death too long to be bumped so easily out of it, even though us getting back together had been what I had longed for, even though it took Sue and me months to find the right 'Third Nuala', and when we did get together with Maria, our new 'Nuala', we established a creatively exciting working relationship. Even though our focused months of rehearsing, writing and doing tiny-venue gigs to get the act back up to speed was hearteningly paying off, and there was the enjoyment of working closely with two top-of-their-game, talented, good-to-be-around women, still it startled me to find I was so low. Work, even loved work, my old saviour, wasn't saviour enough. Besides the obligation to fulfil the two strands of work I loved doing – writing my weekly newspaper column and The Nualas – all I longed for was the proxy death of sleep. My first waking thought, still, was suicide, resolved though I was against it; it was the stalking idea throughout every day, the notion my head sank into the pillow with each night – and whenever I could lie down throughout the day. I needed to nap just to function. I was so fatigued by the death fight in the head. Yet every time my head hit the pillow, for a rest, my inner survivor niggled, 'If you snooze, you lose.'

When I got the cancer diagnosis, there was a huge relief in the realisation that the fatigue may have been down to the disease; the relief of physical malady, beyond just the hateful all-in-the-head of depression. Also, there was an undeniable shadow of relief that now it might be out of my hands. The life I so struggled with might come to an end through entirely different means, and there would be nothing I could do to stop it. The diseased body was in sync with the unhappy head. It made sense to me that I had a cancer all over my heart and that I might die. That I certainly would die if I didn't submit to treatment.

But I did submit to treatment! I did 'go with it'. I was in the system, being shunted along by kind experts, who were intent on life. The world comes into formation around you when such a disease occurs. In the context of what I'd previously experienced, it was delightful. Cry,

'Depression', and expect to provoke instinctive recoil in others; say, 'I have cancer', and know at least there will be a modicum of support and goodwill. Oh, cancer, excuse de luxe that masked the deeper malaise, the worse one.

And here I was, beautiful irony of extraordinary life, being methodically poisoned to kill off the thing that could kill me. So maybe I didn't want to die. 'You can't truly know until you're about to draw your last breath, and by then it's too late to think, yes, I want to live,' someone said to me. I went along with the process. Relieved, at the very least, for the 'time out' it allowed.

16. Eugoogly for a Tumour

I don't doubt that being positive is the best mental state for getting things done in the world. But I think the case for a positive mental mind-set in curing cancer is overstated. If you really bought into that, wouldn't you feel guilt if you found yourself weeping, being angry, being depressed at your diagnosis, at the protracted treatment and the way it affects your body, your daily life, your circumstances, your vision of your future? 'I can't feel these things, they're sickening me,' you'd be telling yourself. 'Goddamn it, gotta tell myself I'm well, I'm good, yippedy-do-dah. Gotta see that baddie, negativity, off at the pass.' What a weird way to experience your humanity – to believe that you're killing yourself by feeling what you feel, which, logically, is probably going to be those emotions along the spectrum of grief.

'At least do positive visualisations,' some may say, like the woman I met who claimed her relative had more or less positively visualised her way out of seemingly terminal ovarian cancer. But is the flip side that negative visualisation would impact as death? Not in my experience. Because, shaming as it is to say it, in the context of all the incredible treatment I was blessed to be given, I did, many times, will the visible mass of tumour to stay and grow. Many times I saw it spread, willed it to spread, like toxic rivers through me, to lungs, bones, liver, brain. Never did I hate it, never did I feel, as I heard others express, that I wanted it removed from my body ASAP, or that having to live with the growth while embarking on pre-operative chemotherapy was a trial.

My cancer was of me. It was telling me something I wanted to embrace. I didn't hate my cancer. I simply didn't. I didn't stoke the feeling. Neither did I deny it. It just curled itself around me night after cancer night: I want to die, I want to die, I want to die. The tumour rested on my heart like comfort, even as I went along with the amazing medicine of it being killed. There was no fight in me. I had absolutely no sense of battling cancer. Neither did I forgo the opportunities of hospital and give in to the imminent death my disease undeniably offered without treatment. My beautiful disease, blooming on my breast, making perfect sense, my tired body, my soul-manifest, easing me as my spirit wished to the longed-for white light of life-exit, and eternal, long longed-for peace. I wept at the news the main tumour was finally visibly responding to chemotherapy – and they weren't tears of relief.

But what would have been my reaction if instead, before that seventh session of chemotherapy, the oncologist had said, 'It's not responding at all, it's not looking good, sorry'?

Being worn down by the months of chemo, I didn't mega-analyse any of my response. I just accepted it, like a reed in a quick river on a windy day – what can you do but flow with it, flex with your fate?

That's life. I was, after all, still living, still getting on with it.

And was, through it all, I could see, dead bloody lucky.

17. Lady Writer

A big issue for many people going through cancer is making the ends meet. What if you're flattened by treatment? What if post-treatment complications mean *finito* for you and your means of earning a livelihood? Given my work, I could keep going. Doing The Nualas, and the other job, dearly beloved that had been my baseline work for several years; I am a newspaper columnist. I became one by a most serendipitous route.

They say luck is when preparation meets opportunity. They also say Pisces is not a lucky sign. In moments of sloppy thinking, I'd find the answer to the ongoing question of my life – Jesus H. Christ, why does everything always have to be such a fucking struggle? – in those two statements. Look, they cancel each other out: no matter how hard you work, you try, you commit to what you do, if you ain't gonna get even a sprinkle of the fairy dust of luck, it ain't gonna happen. Then it did, once, with The Nualas. What an aberration, because wasn't I lack-of-luck personified?

Then *the* most amazingly lucky thing happened, again.

In the midst of juggling means of making a living post The Nualas number one, before The Nualas number two, I'd written a couple of novels. One got published. I thought it would be, like you do, a break. Come January 2007, advance and related book cash depleted, it was clear, as per pretty normal in these things, that that wasn't going to happen. I was back to serious make-money conundrums. In the midst of which one day I got a call from a journalist planning a photo shoot that would feature Irish female comediennes. Would I like to be part of it? Would I fuck, I thought, but didn't say. Grumpy about my flat-lining book career, wary of yet another lazy media spread on the why-so-few-folk-with-ovaries-in-comedy cliché theme and, furthermore, being low on confidence, I was about to say, 'No,' in a fucky-off voice. But the instinct always to say 'Yes' rose up, and it was said despite myself.

So it was I rolled up to a photo studio in Ringsend, Dublin, and spent the following couple of hours shouting, '*Nooo*' (silently, inside). There was styling and coiffuring to be done before the snap was taken. Fashion-backward styling, and hair from the genre 'For sure the brain beneath the scalp will hate it'.

I was rammed into a frothy dress. 'You look lovely,' the journo/stylist said.

'No, I don't. I look like Derek Davis in drag,' I screamed (silently inside).

A girl appeared, with boiling tongs. After five minutes of scorching the head off me, I was left looking like a clown. When she'd started, my hair was slightly Louise

Brooks but totally Tommy Cooper by the end. And then the makeup – vigorously applied, to say the least: she plastered my face like it was a colouring book and she was a toddler with big silly crayons. Suffice it to mention my eyes: I think she might have been going for 'badger' but ended up with 'coal miner staring out of long dark shaft'. I was so shocked when I saw myself in the mirror I couldn't even think up the remark I wasn't going to make.

In the studio the cameraman magicked me into a variety of astounding positions. 'Good girl,' he kept saying, as I smiled into his lens like an idiot – at least my expression matched my hair. 'Pelvis to the wall, chest round to me, more, more, more – good girl,' the man said. What is this, a shoot or a medical? I thought but didn't … I was perched on five-inch stilettos, twisted into a variety of poses best described as 'sciatica'. He got his shot and I got cramp in my foot.

And just as the day was feeling like a hole I had dug, climbed into, and was self-shoving full of muck, I got chatting to the journo/stylist. Who, ten minutes into the conversation, suddenly went, 'Hang on, my editor's looking for a columnist, and I think you'd be perfect.' Within an hour I was on the phone to that editor. The following day I'd filed two potential columns. Five minutes after that I had my favourite job ever, after The Nualas – or, actually, with The Nualas: it's on a par.

Having spent the bones of three years writing prose, one book under the bed, another book in the shops, to have the delight of a tight few hundred words a week published and paid for was beyond a delight. And not to overload on the theme of disastrous photo shoots, but having secured the column, I did another photo shoot for the picture to go with it, on my by-line, and because I was going through a protracted phase of really awful full-length shots – i.e., I was overweight – the initial notion of six hundred words and full-length picture became nine hundred with a head shot when the editor saw the pictures. There's a Chinese proverb somewhere that matches the negative-that-was-actually-positive of this scenario ... somewhere.

Four and a half years into doing the column, cancer came, and it seemed natural to write about it, even though I'd generally veered off being so overtly personal in my writing until then. (Even though, actually, that had been my remit when I got the contract.) There was no big decision involved: I couldn't stop doing my weekly column – it was my living. And I could think of little else but the sudden bombardment of medical experience that was upon me. Maybe it was indulgent; maybe a suspect genre of medico-confessional-catastrophe writing; maybe it would make others, suffering in worse ways, angry at my paid-for national-newspaper weekly outlet; maybe I had become another annoying zit of a Z-list celeb dumping their pus in the press; maybe it was all just pathetic, and cumulatively poised to do me no good in the long term. If there'd be a long term. Whatever, I managed to muster enough what-the-fuckness to plough on.

And those columns got more response than any of the 230-odd others I'd written, nay, carefully crafted to the best of my ability, over the preceding four and a half years. Emails, cards, letters, samples of curative seaweed powders and recipes for cottage cancer curatives came to me. I had touched a public nerve by exposing my private issue. That was more scary than gratifying – it felt like leaving a door open, through which bad could come at me as powerfully as good. More powerfully, for doesn't the bad always leave the deeper mark? A man wrote once to say he hoped my cancer killed me. He was annoyed that I'd been disparaging of then Irish presidential candidate, Dana. What is it about fundamentalist Christians? They're often so – what's the word? Unchristian.

And people, mostly just the odd man, screeched all my doubts back at me in personal, searingly angry prose. Who did I think I was? Their bodies were battlefields of cancer-op scars; their lives were emasculated; their pains real and protracted. I knew nothing by comparison. I was deeming that the banality of my mere stage-three breast version of cancer mattered more than others, by rendering it endlessly in words. Why didn't I smash the mirror of self-reflection, peer through the shards at real suffering – *and shut up*?

I'm paraphrasing what was sent to me in anger because I cannot bear to look back at those emails. There was dread at the opening of every one of the hundreds I got because of the small-percentage probability that it might spew hate. I would rather have had overall silence than that fear. The fundamental anger often seemed to be at the lack of opportunity the sender had to scream out their fear and pain to any hearer within the realm of their life. At the very least, I comforted myself in times of doubt,

I'm some use as a punchbag for festering anger that may have little other release.

I expressed those doubts in a column thus:

What else might I address? Ireland's chances in the rugby world cup? What do I know about rugby, except that it involves two hordes of hunks stampeding into each other, which must be dangerous? Like cancer. There is, of course, this year's Dublin Fringe Theatre Festival, one more exciting week of shows left – haven't checked, but I wonder are any based on the uncontrolled growth of abnormal human cells, also known as cancer? There's also the massive exhibition of cutting-edge international art, Dublin Contemporary 2011, in venues across the capital until 31 October. In the Royal Hibernian Academy, Lisa Yuskavage's paintings of ladies with fantastical curves and enormous nude bosoms are causing a stir. Which reminds me, I've got …

Oh, well, there you go. I tried. But wow, cancer, cancer, cancer. You're like that Kylie Minogue song, 'Can't Get You out of My Head'. She also had … you know yourself.

Ultimately, good outweighed the bad, and the communication underlined something I was keenly aware of throughout: my privileged position.

Here, a short compendium of some quotes from that sharing:

I understand what it's like to face the prospect of a Mastectomy ... As it transpired I was told by my doctor that my B. C. was so advanced (metastatic in the Liver) it was too late for a mastectomy, there was 'no point mutilating the body'. I am still here nearly four years later, going to Daycare Oncology for drug treatments and tests every three weeks.

I have to take Tamoxifen every day for 5 years. I hate having to take a tablet every day. I feel I have put on weight ... however, if it does what it is supposed to do I guess it's ok.

You didn't mention that your prosthesis has a mind of its own and can end up under your chin! Very bad if you are doing River Dance and you get beaten to death by a bit of wobbly plastic.

If I had to do it again I would have the reconstruction done at a later date.

I won't use the word brave, I'm sure you're sick of it. I'm three years over mine and the word always annoyed me, we don't have a choice, we have to fight it or lie down and die.

This is a subject that needs to be discussed in the open – too many people feel they are alone.

Over the past few months I have been reading your column ... This was me. This was happening to me. I too went through chemo. I sat while someone shaved my head. And the weirdest thing of all I walked to theatre to have my breast removed. I'm crying again now typing this!!!! God I'm getting on my own nerves now. Fed up of crying.

Like you I hate the pink bunny picture.

As a GP I deal with cancer on a daily basis. After your first article revealing your diagnosis, one 30 year old patient read about your devastating news. It prompted her visit to me ... She was diagnosed with early stage breast cancer – there is no doubt in my mind that she has you to thank for saving her life. As doctors we can only do our best to educate and be informative in a compassionate and honest manner. However – it is much more compelling if one hears one's personal experience.

I just want it all over before my boy's Holy Communion at the end of April, but now it's not.

One of the most stupid things I had said to me was that God chose me to have the cancer as I had a loving husband and four loving normal children to help me cope – so if my husband drank and came home and beat me up and my children were all on drugs and in Mountjoy I would not have been chosen? Give me strength woman.

I got an appointment for a check-up for April, which will be seven months after my mastectomy. Gosh, it's strange how all the fear comes back again.

I have fibro cystic breast disease and have mammograms and biopsies every 3 months. If I've had one needle I must have had 100 by now!! I'm returning this Friday for the usual striptease and craic. It's like walking into a scene from Cheers at this stage, everybody knows my name! Over the years I've met so many women sitting in waiting areas, sometimes in silence, sometimes in tears ... There's always worry attached ... especially the week of waiting for biopsy [results]. It's not easy explaining this to friends.

You'll get used to it [wearing the compression sleeve] like you get used to being bald, being titless or having a silicone implant that's kinda crawling upwards so I have a boob which is empty. I will get another operation done to get them to fix it when I am ready.

Now I can look back on that dreadful time as being a Great Learning Curve in my life.

I was diagnosed with breast cancer last Summer ... I'm 47, married with two young children and my whole life fell apart in seconds. Luckily I have been given a good prognosis too but it doesn't wipe out the fear and the sheer terror of that day in the breast care clinic.

Anne Gildea

It brought my family closer together.

I was diagnosed with breast cancer at the grand age of 38 over 3 years ago ... Two of my best friends were also diagnosed, all of us young and with no family history. I really feel that it has somehow become trivialised. I had one man say to me 'oh everyone has that these days' when we told him and I was just gobsmacked. It is tough, tough, tough. I agree with your analogy that it's [a mastectomy] akin to an amputation.

An old lady said to me 'from the day you're born, you're born to the hearse, you may think you're bad, you could be worse' and that applies to all of us.

Tonight I'm in tears as your column reminded me of my Dad and the journeys he had through the corridors of St James. I miss him so much. Family is everything, you know this.

18. A Wait

'The mastectomy is a breeze after the chemo,' a woman who'd been through both told me. A bit like saying that having your leg sawn off is better than being shot in the head, but you dig the positive where you can. People I met kept indicating reasons to be cheerful. Stories of friends of friends delighted with refreshed cleavages, 'tummy tucks' from where tissue for new breasts had been removed, of remaining breasts lifted to match pert new ones, natty tattooed-on nipples, speedy recoveries, and women, eventually, not noticing any difference! 'My mother said no to reconstruction initially, then her swimming prosthesis floated away in the pool and that was it. New boob, never looked back.' There was the delight when a reconstructed woman slept with a new man for the first time and, joy of joys, 'he didn't notice anything'.

The focus in general social chit-chat was on what was gained, the cosmetic replacement, not on the loss. That was the way I wanted to look at it too: mastectomy was inevitable, a common surgical procedure, the removal of tissue non-essential to your biological functioning. And it could be replaced with an updated edition. Compared to the complications other internal or systemic cancers presented, I'd won the lotto of cancer.

After the last chemo, there was a three-week wait to see the surgeon. I felt anxiously excited. I was impatient. It seemed for ever. At that appointment I would be given the date for the operation. Then suddenly I was there. Back where it had begun, in the breast care clinic where, four months previously, I'd first been told I had cancer, that a mastectomy was inevitable.

Since then I'd been in innumerable 'Just pop your top off' situations. Here we were again. What formerly had only been touched by another human being in an intimate scenario had been, in the previous months, thoroughly exposed to and manhandled by so many medically: doctors, technicians, radiologists, consultants; surgical, oncological, radiation. Because I wasn't in a relationship with anyone, I'd come to see my breast solely in terms of 'medical problem'. I'd become disassociated from the animal reality of the surgery that was about to happen – Leftie was about to leave the building, without me attached.

Examining the breast, the surgeon said she could feel no evidence of the tumour. There was a possibility that after the operation no remaining cancer would be found, she said. But they still had to remove it. Did I understand? Yes, I said, I did. Some women found that difficult, she noted. Yes, but I could see it was positive that the tissue could be tested to see how your body had responded to chemotherapy, which obviously wasn't the case when mastectomy came first. Yes, it was all good. The area would be completely flat after. Did I understand that? Yes, I said, I did. One straight neat scar, she reiterated. OK.

She mentioned that the possibility of immediate reconstruction had been discussed at the team meeting that morning. (In Ireland, under the 'centre of excellence' system, all the breast care specialists, radiologists, oncologists, surgeons, nurses, meet to go through each case before each stage of treatment is decided.) It wasn't possible, because of the subsequent radiation I was to have. I already knew that, but it was reassuring that it had been mentioned, that reconstruction was taken as essential and offered as part of the mastectomy treatment. An appointment would be made for me to see the cosmetic surgeon before the mastectomy.

Then I got the date I'd long awaited: 2 December. A Friday. I did a quick calculation. It was eighteen days away. Bummer: another couple of weeks of ticking days off. That was all I was thinking about at that time: the time.

There was suddenly a shift. The reality of what was soon to happen hit home. The breast care nurse asked was I up to seeing the prosthesis I'd be given post-op. Of course. Why not? We went into a tiny room, more of a glorified cupboard. She, my sister and I were huddled close together on chairs. She took out an array of little things: the flesh-coloured silicone breast shapes, like the proverbial chicken fillets, with a small risen nipple bump, a shadow of my natural 'coat peg'. I held it in my hand. My substitute breast would be the same as this. It had a soft backing, and was filled with stuff like you'd use to pack a teddy. I'd have this type for the first few weeks, while the wound was still tender. Then I'd be given a slightly heavier version, composed entirely of silicone.

She showed us the prosthesis bra, with internal pockets for such artificial breasts. She packed the breast shape in, handed it to me: a bra not to support a breast but be a breast. She showed us a length of narrow clear plastic tubing, two of these would be poking out of the wound post-op, she explained. They were the 'drains'. They'd have plastic bulbs attached, to collect the blood and fluid that would issue from the wound. It was the physicality of these things, holding, touching, seeing them, that for the first time connected me to the impending reality. Had I been in denial?

No, the mind handles what comes as you go through the whole unnatural sequence of treatment. Why would this have been forefront when I'd been absorbed in the ups and downs of chemotherapy from 20 July to 26 October? Now 2 December was the new D Day. Or should that be B Day? Breast literally, completely, off.

'I'm just left with the image of half a chest. Suddenly the grief at losing my breast is almost unbearable. I'm physically sick, shaking, crying, thinking about it,' I wrote in my diary.

A few days later I had a meeting with the cosmetic

surgeon so that he could see my chest as it soon wouldn't be: complete. At length he described the various options. One involving taking fat from the stomach sounded best. The surgeon had also mentioned that that was the one the team considered most appropriate. He measured my breasts, the distance from clavicle bone to nipple, a distance that would have started out at twenty-one centimetres, was now twenty-seven. Ageing drift – 'When you're young you automatically associate your breasts with the upper part of your body,' I used to say onstage. 'Could you make the new one more pert, and lift the old one?' I asked. Though 'pert' probably isn't the correct cosmetic-surgical terminology. What is – 'pointy-uppy'? He could, because I was DD and the biggest size he reconstructed to was a C cup, he said.

The operation to lift and reduce the old and balance the new would take place at least six months after the reconstruction so he could see how the new breast had settled on the body, he explained. Then he needed to see the stomach, where the tissue for the new breast would come from. To quantify it he sat in front of me. I pulled down my knickers a bit and he held a wodge of belly with his two hands, figuring its fatty volume. I don't know the technical name for this examination but it could be called 'humiliation maxima'. 'Lean forward,' he instructed, and I was so discombobulated by the situation, I leaned diagonally towards him. 'No,' he clarified, 'from the waist.' Oh, yeah, of course. God, I felt stupid. Is it a good or bad thing he's a bit attractive, I found myself wondering, as he medically tugged at the bit of my body I'd always been most self-conscious about: my not-hard belly. Then he squashed around the belly button and noted that that was where they'd be harvesting the tissue for the breast. I looked down at my body and tried to see it as he did, as a medical specimen. But I took the fact he said, 'In terms of breast reconstruction you have a small stomach,' as a compliment.

In case I was thinking of the operation as a handy proxy tummy tuck, he noted that fat either side would remain. 'Oi, what "fat either side"? Wot ya on about?' I didn't respond, because (1) I don't speak in crap mock-*EastEnders*, and (2) I figured attempted flirty informality was inappropriate. The minimum wait was six months post-radiation to have reconstruction; to ensure optimal healing, even longer was advisable, he was saying. 'It's not about the breast, it's about you,' he concluded, advising me not to be in a mad dash to have it done. It all seemed far in the future anyway. Would I even want to bother by then, having actually been through mastectomy?

I watched a film about breast cancer: one of the women featured said her reconstructed breast felt like 'a lump of steak on my body'. She couldn't bear to touch it: doing so reminded her of what was lost. I'm just balancing my perspective, I figured, boning up on the negatives. I met other women who had had the operation I was going to have, and all were delighted with the results, the new mound of breast, the flattened stomach, the feeling of being restored to a more normal 'new normal'. I was shown long red lower-belly scars that women assured me didn't bother them at all. What they'd been given in return was so heartening. Such positivity was very powerful.

There was also the issue of the lymph nodes. I was used to instructors in the Bikram yoga classes I attended noting that there was 'more lymph in the body than blood' before engaging in postures designed to help flush it around the multifarious channels of the lymphatic system. The lymph nodes were components of that system, which runs complementary to the bloodstream, draining fluid and debris from the tissue. All three levels of nodes in the breast area would be removed, from the armpit up to the clavicle bone, a linear network of little pip-like vessels. There could be anything from fifteen to thirty; the number varies from body to body. Without them the arm could get lymphoedema, meaning that matter that should have drained remained in the tissue, resulting in swelling. It could get chronic: the arm could blow up like a puffy cushion. You had to be careful ever after with too much exertion, heavy lifting, getting cuts on the arm or stings. There might be ongoing pain, dimpling, compromised mobility, numbness. You might need to wear a full-arm compression sleeve, a glove, even. It was recommended you wore the sleeve every time you had to fly, regardless of arm swelling. The surgeon had been reassuring that the possibility of such complications was small. Eventually other nodes remaining would compensate. Probably.

'The way to look at it is, your breast wasn't a good friend to you so it had to go,' a woman at a cancer support centre told me. She was dealing with the loss of her own breast, in the throes of chemotherapy: bald, down, but getting through it because what else are you going to do?

People use the word 'brave'. 'You're so brave,' they say, and it's so irritating. What's the flip side of 'being brave' in this situation? That someone might say to you, 'Excuse me, I don't think you're being brave enough'? Bravery doesn't come into it. It's illness, it's a fact of life, you deal with it. I could see that the woman wasn't convinced by her bad-friend theory even as she uttered it.

I wasn't either. Before cancer, I think I'd fallen out of love with my body a bit. I reminded myself of that line from comedienne Sarah Millican, to the effect, 'Is it a compliment when you go to bed with someone for the first time and they say, "Oh, your breasts are so lovely and long"?' Gravity had been working its tricks on my chest: what formerly had been the embodiment of 'perky' had become 'pendulous and a bit huge'.

But my left breast wasn't a bad friend: it was half of the pair I'd had since I was ten. I developed early. I remember being mortified when one day a younger girl came up to me in the schoolyard, stood way too close and, shockingly, touched them. She pressed each of my chest lumps in turn, unselfconsciously marvelling at their feel and mass. 'Do you wear a bra?' she asked, in a strong London accent. She'd recently moved back to Ireland from England: it would never have occurred to an Irish kid to be so forward.

'No. I do not,' I stuttered, burning red with the shame of the question.

'Just asking.' She shrugged and walked away, leaving me with embarrassment compounded by a sense that my answer had been stupid. Really my answer ought to have been 'Mitts off, pig-face' but I didn't talk that way. Or simply 'Yes, actually, I am currently sporting an ill-fitting, puke yellow, front-fastening cast-off from a teen cousin in Manchester. It's not quite right, but it does the trick.' But I didn't talk that way either.

My first bras weren't great. Well-worn, small-cupped lacy items that came in parcels from our cousins in England. Grey-white, obscure blue, manky yellow, indefinite shades suggestive of the mistaken mixed wash. Frivolous original shades that might have appealed to their teenage original owners.

I wasn't yet a teen, and I was uncomfortable with the blooming bustiness of my familiar flat chest. I read about mums going to the shops with their daughters to purchase an item called a 'training bra', which seemed a bit over the top. You don't need training tights to figure out how to 'wear' twin long woolly stockings joined at the top, so why the big deal with the fairly-obvious-how-it-goes-on double cup of the bra? But it seemed the moment of bust-beginning required a mother-daughter moment because the arrival of breasts announced unequivocally, I Am Woman. Your body was drawing attention to itself.

I had the first bust on the block among my school friends, attracting the first of 'those kind of glances' from not just boys but men. It made me tremendously uncomfortable. Then I learned to love my lady-lumps. Then I was miffed when they drooped, the cycle of life from a cleavage point of view. Now I was about to lose one: an unexpected blip in the script.

Funnily enough, shortly before diagnosis I had decided

a few really fine bras were in order. The woman who measured me in Arnotts of Henry Street chose a couple of French ones with price tags as handsome as the cleavage they gave me – 'Because I'm worth it,' I told myself. Shortly after, the swelling that eventually brought me to the cusp of breast removal became evident, growing large in a short space of time. They were hardly worn because they squashed what had become a painful inflammation.

As the technician manoeuvred my left breast onto the mammogram plate for the post-chemo/pre-operative scan, it was hard to believe there was anything wrong. The poison had worked its tumour-munching magic and my breast looked completely normal again – even though it was being flattened in a device that reminded me of a tool shed vice grip. It didn't hurt like it had before, when the tumour could be felt and the machine plates pressed the hell out of it.

Then it was into the ultrasound room, to lie boobs akimbo on the examination table. Another medic, a lovely radiology consultant, explained in detail what the muddy images on her screen indicated: nodes completely responded, three areas of suspect tissue in the breast remaining. Finally she reiterated what had been established from the get-go: full mastectomy. What could I say? Goodbye, old friend.

I thought about the chest in its sexual dimension: bazoomas, jugs, melons, titties, all the silly, erotic, affectionate terms. Memories of hands holding them, the squashing, weighing, wobbling, appreciative kneading, being kissed. The audacity of someone new touching you so intimately, the naughtiness of 'You've got great tits': sex. The last thing on my mind now, I couldn't imagine ever wanting to do it again.

The wait for the op seemed interminable. I was offered a course of acupuncture at a cancer support centre I occasionally attended. That wouldn't usually be my thing, I'm not a needle fan (who is?), but I thought, Why not? A relaxing distraction, I figured. Indeed! In the perfectly warm therapy room there was the plinkety-plonk of just-so-loud relaxation music, and an oil burner wafting lovely aromatherapy pong, and I was invited to get up on the comfy therapy bed by a charming handsome chap of a therapist, who, I decided, must be expert in the acupuncture, given he was needling cancer people such as me. WRONG, I realised too late, after twenty minutes of ouching as he inserted multiple long, long needles, each startlingly sore. 'Please, just take them all out,' I entreated eventually, as they continued to throb. And as he complied, every released needle point poured blood. My body looked like a rendition of St Sebastian's. And the therapist's waste basket was soon full of the bloodied tissues he'd desperately patted on the blood. 'Are you new to this by any chance?' I asked, too late. The answer was yes. He was training; it was a sideline. 'Oh, what's your main job?' I wondered.

'I'm a butcher,' he revealed.

No kidding.

I went into overdrive Googling again, prior to the mastectomy, getting lists of searches with notes like 'You have visited this site seventeen times before'. There was nothing left to read, nothing I wanted to reread an eighteenth time. Then I discovered startlingly graphic operation films available on YouTube. The clearest and most detailed one I found was made strange by a Richard Clayderman-type piano ditty that had been added as a soundtrack. Mastectomy and Muzak: who thought up that combo? The worst was of a Russian surgeon in action – less 'modified radical mastectomy', more 'gore-fest featuring robust Slavic scalpel and unfortunate female chest'. I watched each many times.

It amazed me how easily skin separated from tissue when a scalpel was applied with appropriate pressure. How neatly the whole mound could be incised away from the muscle of the chest wall. How fiddly it would be to access the local lymph nodes and remove all of them, avoiding arteries, nerves and whatever else it's essential to avoid damaging in the process. How your sleep-dead arm would be held back by surgical assistants to allow access to the armpit nodes, the cutting and snipping of your inner tissue. All of it, breasts and nodes, sundered from your body, rendered a 'tissue sample', a mass of blood and fat, taken up by hands in bloodied translucent white gloves, plopped in some manner of sterile container, with its ellipse of white skin, nipple on top. Labelled and forwarded to a hospital laboratory. How weird, how fascinating. I wished I could be awake to see it. How empowered and engaging to be a surgeon, playing God with the human body.

That was the way I processed what was about to happen, by going over and over every detail, as if doing so would erase any impending, potential grief.

'What a crazy world,' I wrote in my diary. 'Three trillion videos of Justin Bieber, and I could only find two on complete axillary clearance. I want nodes, not a kiddie-man who looks like his life revolves round hairdryers. And when I Google, looking for an image of lymph nodes, why does a picture of Prince Charles appear?'

I got up early the morning I was due into the hospital, hadn't slept. I did a yoga class, phoned the hospital to see if there was a bed available. The receptionist said she'd have to call me back, and would do so at two p.m. Another wait! She called bang on and, as I had been assured, there was a bed available. I had to check in by four thirty. I put the phone down and burst into tears. I couldn't articulate exactly why I was crying. If I'd asked myself, the answer would have been, 'What's the freaking problem? Aren't you being looked after? So just get on with it!' The waiting, an hour and a half till it was time for my old chum Sue to come, pick up Una and me, and drive us to the hospital.

Soon we were rolling into the underground car park; we were in the lift up; we were walking across the main concourse; I was signing the forms at Admissions. Everything was now simultaneously dream-like and hyper-real. No matter the statistics stating how many women have this done: when it's happening to you it's a full-on head-mash.

Signed in, we were off again, round a curve of shiny corridor, up in another lift, pushing through double doors and into another world. The surgery ward, a microclimate in the ordinary atmosphere of things. It was hot, the air redolent of antiseptic, cleaning agents and recent patient meals. There were beds on wheels, medical accoutrements, laundry bags of sheets, utility rooms with shelves of meds and bedpans, prone patients and bustling nurses in blue, one of whom told us, 'Wait.' We sat in a tiny closed-off waiting room by the entrance to the ward. After thirty minutes we were being shown not just 'a bed' but a room. I'd drawn a long straw in the lottery of our two-tier health system: I'd got a Private Room. Mini yippee.

'Fasting,' a sign on the door said.

Two junior doctors, a girl and a guy, came in on the night round. They said the operation was scheduled for the following lunchtime. There were some tests, a consent form to sign. The female doctor marked a large 'L' in a circle on the breast to be removed, with a purple indelible pen. 'We do that whenever pairs of body parts are involved,' she explained. They left. I remarked to my sister that I felt like a branded cow. 'I'd be happier if they stuck a flag in it,' she replied. My brother and two friends visited too. It was a veritable party in the room that night.

The nurses kindly allowed the visitors stay past official visiting hours. Eventually alone, I was offered a sleeping tablet, which I took – first time ever I'd felt the need for such an item. I fancied oblivion until the time for the deed arrived.

Cows – that was where sleeping-pill thoughts drifted before sleep.

I was back in Sligo. It was 1983, on the awful morning the cows were suddenly all being taken away for sale.

It was a small herd and we'd pet names for each, White Heady, Mrs Tumnus, Kinnegad a few. If you've ever known cows you'd appreciate each had her own quirks, what you might call 'personality'. And all had a slow bovine motherliness. I remembered the sickening sounds of that morning, hearing the cattle truck come at dawn to bring them to the mart; the hoofs of the animals shifting uncertainly on the rough surface of the yard outside; them being belted with sticks and shouted at as they were driven up the wooden ramp. And then thinking of their journey to Ballymote in the crowded truck; their soft bellies would have pressed together as they struggled to keep balance while the truck negotiated the narrow roads; their udders mashing twixt their trembling legs. Then the noise and bustle of the mart; the gangs of capped farmers come with cattle to sell; the buyers, long-ash cigarettes hanging from their lips, eyeing cattle as walking meat; and all the animals, mooing with anxiety, corralled in concrete pins, waiting for their turn under the auctioneer's hammer. The auctioneer then chanting the bids, as our dear cows circled under the eyes of whoever was buying; the final belt of the hammer, 'Sold!' and the sad last journey to the abattoir, the smell of death making the good cows' eyes wide with terror, as men in blood- and shit-stained white overalls lined them up for the stun gun, and they ended the twelve summers of their milky lives strung upside-down on moving hooks.

I was swaying with everything sad as the clock clicked on to the Big Day.

19. Breast Off

The following morning the operation outfit was delivered: surgical gown, compression stockings, long and white, like thin football socks, and disposable knickers. I put off putting them on. Mid-morning my surgeon popped down, dressed in green scrubs. She was between operations. 'You know why we have to do this today?' she asked, reiterating, reassuring. She asked to check the breast one last time, and I opened my pyjama top. As she talked, she spontaneously did-up the three buttons I'd undone. There was something so caring, so human, in that small automatic gesture. It was so reassuring, indicative of the respect she would show my body, even though I was one of many breast patients in her ongoing busy schedule.

Some time later an orderly told me to put on my surgery get-up, and suddenly things speeded up. The gurney arrived and I sat on it. Then I was pushed out into a warren of hospital corridors, trying, mentally, to slow time, to hold onto each increment of the long-awaited bizarre experience. As you're wheeled along, your eyes are a tracking shot, shiny linoleum floors, blue double doors, winter light bouncing off white walls – left and left and left again the gurney was pushed, to a final left through two sets of double doors.

I was in the surgery 'holding area'. There was a crucifix on the wall above the reception desk. There were a couple of other people on gurneys, waiting, a small white artificial Christmas tree, sporting a smattering of shiny baubles, against the wall. Christmas was coming, I'd forgotten. Details were rechecked, there was a slight issue over a pregnancy test that hadn't been done. 'Believe me, if I am it's the Immaculate Conception,' I said, getting into the festive mood. They had to get clearance that the operation could proceed.

Then another wheeling, towards the theatre, my mind racing. I felt desperate to grasp what was happening. Me in half-naked clothes under a thin blanket, vulnerable: I wanted to control it by knowing everything – every related scientific abstract involved; the science, the personnel, the procedure; every taste, texture, smell, sound and sight. I wanted to suck it all in. I'd waited so long for this to happen and now it was going so fast. I wanted to honour it, the personal enormity of the slicing off of my breast, in the context of a place where human breasts are sliced off week in, week out. I didn't want to feel I was just another one, even as I knew I was.

I thought of the evolution of this operation, the hellish sensations, the unconscionable pain of those women who had undergone it in past times without anaesthetic. How must they have felt, their desire to live so strong, facing into such new butchery?

Then we were in the small bright theatre antechamber, with a plethora of introductions and sudden flurry of activity around me, like I was a Formula 1 car in a race pit stop: the smiling registrar, who would assist with the surgery; a medical man who delicately attached small monitor pads to my body; another who asked about my dental work, 'Because I'm going to put a tube with a metal end down your throat and it might hit off your teeth.' He then pricked a cannula in the back of my right hand, for the anaesthetic: more sharp pain, which I'd got used to. And the anaesthetist, tall, friendly – attractive, I even noted in my silently overwhelmed state.

He had a European accent. He asked, 'What's your favourite drink?'

'Pardon?'

'Just imagine you're drinking a long glass of champagne, Anne,' he said.

I was thinking that I'd marginally prefer frozen vodka, straight, when everything went wobbly, like every film scene you've ever seen of everything going wobbly for someone before – blackout.

Next thing I was being wheeled again, being told, 'This is the recovery room.' Being asked, 'Is there pain?' Yes, there was, burning in my armpit. I looked under the blue gown, they must have taken it off and put it back on in the theatre. Had I been naked? Why did that matter? Too many views of ops on YouTube, the sleeping meat on the surgical table, the vulnerability of it. Through my groggy vision I saw a flattened undulation of flesh where the mound of breast used to be. And a thin white bandage under a long, wide, clear adhesive plaster that was sealed fast to the skin. Indented bulges of cellophane-sealed flesh instead of the breast, clean, neat, flat, weird.

Two clear tubes poked from my armpit, where it would have been dug into to remove the nodes, coloured red with blood, draining into plastic bulbs.

'Is that better?' asked the nurse, injecting liquid into the cannula in my hand.

I started sobbing. 'Sister!' I cried. 'Can someone call my sister?' They wheeled a curtain around me. There were other people recovering who didn't need my sobs, or maybe it was for my privacy. Who cared? I couldn't believe what had been done to me, even as I had known all along it would happen and why. Anger was definitely there: grief and anger. The anaesthetist appeared to check that I'd come round. I asked about his accent. He told me where he was from. We shook hands and he said something along the lines of 'sorry to be meeting in this situation', and that one exchange, ad hoc, incidental, so human, meant so much.

As I clambered awkwardly from the gurney onto my hospital bed, hoping the difficult movement wouldn't burst the newly sewn slash across my chest, my sister appeared from behind the curtain over the door to my room. It was bang on seven o'clock, visiting time. Was I ever so relieved to see her? She'd been my witness through all. She sat beside me and cried, which was good, to have the close acknowledgement of it being emotional, however ordinary a mastectomy is in terms of hospital procedure.

I talked at Una for the next four hours. Whatever concoction of meds I was on, I was buzzing from it, on a high. I didn't sleep for the following two nights, and then only with sleeping pills.

The day following surgery was a Saturday. The visiting registrar, in casual scarf and jacket, popped in to say that the surgeon was 'really happy for you' because the operation had gone well. My gut reaction was to scream, though I didn't. I wasn't a calm adult, thinking, Thank you, surgery experts, for saving my life. I was just angry at the thought of this registrar being present at my mutilation. It's illogical, but I resented her get-on-with-life clothes, me in pyjamas, mutilated. I'm just expressing the full negativity of what I felt. I was just thinking of me knocked out, half naked, being cut open the day before. Cancer was out of the equation. All I could think of was losing breast and lymph nodes, the scarred aftermath. And that phraseology 'really happy'! Though I knew what she was saying was positive.

According to the late British writer Christopher Hitchens, who had recently died from his cancer, martinis are like breasts: one is one too few while three is one too many. And now I was a one-martini, trying to grasp the ludicrous reality of having a solo breast.

'You can get a T-shirt saying "My other boob is a boob,"' my brother suggested.

'Some women take days to look at it fully,' a nurse told me.

Aren't I great facing this monstrous reflection full on? I thought. 'Lovely neat scar, successful surgery, I'm very lucky,' I muttered, all logical.

The night before I left hospital I sat on the bed and howled for over an hour into my towel. A night nurse told me, 'I've been doing this job a long time. It won't take days or weeks to come to terms with it. It'll take months.' I knew.

A first drain was removed; the flat tail of it that had rested under the skin was surprising, long. Another thing I recall about the drains was that the bloody fluid that issued from them smelt unpleasant.

I went home to Una's house, intending to head back to my own apartment. I'd a column to write. Instead I crawled into bed and mega-slept. She went off and got the meds. I'd been prescribed painkillers. Later, we watched a programme on telly, an Irish presenter, Joe O'Shea, exploring men's cosmetic surgery. A man who had had a load of work done wanted to get more: 'There's still one thing about his body he's not happy with,' Joe explained.

'Funny if they pulled back and revealed he had one huge ear,' I said to Una. The idea of having surgery for vanity seemed ludicrous.

The wound was painful at night, which I quickly forgot, it healed so well. But this diary entry reminds me: '*12 December, 5.30 a.m.* Another night propped up on pillows afraid to lie down for fear of pain. Pain all across chest, deep, almost makes me stop breathing, deep into armpit, down back of arm. Can't turn over with pain across chest – makes me nervous.'

Why nervous? Probably because I hadn't expected it to be at all painful, so when it was I thought there was something wrong. But it wasn't unbearable. And it certainly didn't last.

The following day, 13 December, I went back to see the surgeon for the results of the laboratory results on the dissected tissue. It was the best possible outcome: the test showed a 'pathologic complete response' (pCR), meaning that there was no trace of cancer in any of the breast or node tissue examined. It could be inferred that the regime of chemotherapy I'd been on pre-operatively had zapped all the cancer that had shown in scans of breast and armpits, and any microscopic offshoot that might have migrated and lodged in the liver or wherever. Therefore I had the best possible prognosis. I didn't think, Yippee, I've beaten cancer. I thought, Wow, they've beaten it. My sister, beside me, was beyond delighted. And now I had some important work to do about being alive.

The post-op pain lessened that day, when the final drain was pulled out after the meeting with the surgeon. The wound had become infected. The slit made in the skin for the drain leaked a fountain of lurid yellow pus, and continued to drain, pour wound-fluid, for another week, which I felt was positive, the wound naturally draining whatever residue was there, in preparation for healing.

The strip of bandage over the breast wound was removed. The nurse told me that the clear crustiness remaining along it wasn't a scab but surgical glue. I wasn't to pick at it: it would fall off gradually of its own accord. I thought it looked as if I'd had half Frankenstein's face grafted to my chest. The sight of it was unreal but not that bad, I told myself. The scar was, as the surgeon had promised, amazingly neat. Compared to the stitching of some mastectomies I'd watched on the Internet, it was a work of art.

A few nights later I attended a fortieth-birthday party. People squeezed my arm the side of operation.

'How are you?'

'You're looking great.'

'I'm grand.' It hurt. Be careful where you touch people who've had surgery. I kept having little weeps alone in the loos. Natural enough, I told myself, whatever the tears are about: part pain, part adjusting to new reality, but you're not sure what that new reality is. And are you being too dramatic, calling it 'a new reality'? I had reasons only to be happy. There was no evidence of cancer remaining, the best possible prognosis. It couldn't have gone better. I'd need no more chemotherapy. I was going to live.

I was given a breast prosthesis and two special bras. In the hospital breast care centre, there was a small room with cupboards full of breasts, bras and several mirrors. An edging of roses was painted here and there on the furniture, a feminine, non-medical touch that indicated, 'Hey, we know there's a mountain of emotion involved in all this.' Indeed. I showed the prosthesis to friends, who were impressed: 'Wow, trannies would kill for a pair of these.'

'It really does looks like chicken.'

It was beautifully soft, so well shaped, a lovely flesh colour.

Later I said to my brother that losing a breast didn't bother me that much.

'You were devastated after the operation!' he said.

'Was I?' I honestly didn't remember. As with childbirth, from what I'd read, you forget the bad bits as soon as it's over. Except with surgery you don't have a child at the end of it.

Just before Christmas I went back to see the oncologist. The waiting room was crowded. I was squashed beside a woman from whom I started getting the whole medical history – 'I had a five-pound tumour removed from my stomach,' she told me. Like someone proud of the largest marrow at the county fair: 'Well, the five-pounder is very impressive but the red rosette goes to Mrs Murphy and the one the size of a turnip in her uterus! Congratulations, Mrs Murphy. Unfortunately Mrs Murphy can't be with us today because she's not with any of us any more.' Perhaps I was getting intolerant of medical-history conversations.

I made a note to self: other than finishing the sixty-minute television documentary that two filmmakers had been making of my 'cancer journey', doing press and radio interviews to promote it because it was to be broadcast on RTÉ One television, prime time, and writing an eighty-thousand-word book based round the experience of getting it, and wrapping up those months of nine-hundred-word columns in a national Sunday newspaper, I was not going to mention my cancer any more. It wasn't going to define me.

That day I also met with the radiotherapy professor who explained that I needed to have the radiation, even though I had had a pCR, because there was a possibility that microscopic amounts of disease remained. Also, because I wanted to have a breast reconstruction, the radiotherapy would ensure, as far as was absolutely possible, that the chest wall was cancer-free before transplanted tissue, or an implant, obscured the area. 'It's the gold standard of treatment,' he said. And I couldn't argue with that.

In January I saw the lymphoedema specialist. I was fortunate that the hospital I attended has such a person. Early-stage intervention, and prevention are essential to stem lymphoedema developing into the chronic, debilitating condition it can become, for which there is no cure. A poster on the wall showed, step by step, how to layer a compression bandage the length of a leg hugely swollen with lymphoedema. The caption at the bottom of the poster read: 'Jobst – Comfort, Health, Style'. Marketing palaver even applied to serious-condition big-bandaging. I loved it.

The specialist made many tiny marks down my arm on the side of the cancer, measuring, terribly precise. He noted that it was a few millimetres thicker in the lower half than it was on the right. 'But that's not a problem,' he said. Then he did a short lymphatic massage, light feathery movements, first at the base of my neck, to open the lymph channels there, then sweeping gradually up the length of the affected arm to the armpit and across the clavicle bone towards where he had begun.

The delicacy of his touch was extremely relaxing. 'I could fall asleep as you're doing that,' I told him.

He said he had one patient who always fell asleep. 'But

better the patient falls asleep than the therapist.'

There was also an appointment with a physio who showed me exercises to get arm movement back; how to massage the arm, and the wound, to help healing. Cords had developed in my armpit and down my arm: sinuous lines of tissue, tight under the skin. Lymph vessels that had atrophied, I read on the Internet. 'They will gradually resolve of their own accord,' she said. Meanwhile they made the arm rather tight and difficult to move.

A correspondent to one of my columns wrote to inform me about 'casting for recovery'. What's this? I wondered. An organisation that helps cancer recovery by trying to get you parts in films and plays? Who could turn you down when it was appealing on your behalf? 'For Christ's sake, she's recovering from stage three breast cancer.'

Directors forced to go: 'OK, OK, she's way too old for the part, but go on, let's hear her rendition of "The Sun Will Come Tomorrow" anyway.'

Alas, no, it was about fishing. Fishing! 'Fly-fishing has been medically accepted as a beneficial sport to help with the physical and mental healing process.' It's a charity that runs fishing retreats for ladies recovering from breast cancer. I thought I might look into it in the future – healing through fish – when I was over the current more inert phase I was in: comfort through chips.

If you were to frame the trio of cancer treatments in S-words, chemo is being 'sick', surgery is feeling 'sore' and radiation should be getting 'sunburned', but the word that actually popped to mind was 'sci-fi', a notion formed from all the impressions that stacked up once

I was in the radiation treatment area: the wide white corridors leading to the large radiation room; the calm white-coated technicians who got me to lie on the hard plinth in front of the massive grey shiny-veneered arch of the machine; the room darkened to allow a grid of green guiding lights be focused to match up with the tiny permanent dots previously tattooed on my body; the smooth grinding sound as the large flat circular metal radiation-delivery device manoeuvred over me, its glass surface reflecting the lights on my body; the technicians gently mooching me this way and that to get an exact position, placing additional marks on me in red ink, as they communicated with each other in numbers: 'Ninety-four point seven, ninety-two, three, one millimetre' – whatever. It was all so alien that I wouldn't really have been surprised if a man with a blue head, lizard eyes and a bony frill across the top of his skull had popped into the room and squeaked, 'OK, measurements good, let's zap,' in an accent that suggested 'intergalactic'.

My treatment was in two areas, chest and base of neck, from three different angles. The rads themselves took just a couple of minutes, but all in, the process took about half an hour when extra images had to be taken, to match my position with the original treatment plan. More regularly, without imaging, it took about fifteen minutes. The extra imaging devices emerged from the main machine on robotic arms, one an overhead box with a flat lens, another a large grey plastic panel that appeared from the side. It was quite astonishing.

Side effects were reddening, hardening and tightening

across the operation scar, giving me the feeling of being slightly cooked. It was, as everyone told me, 'the easy part' relative to the other treatments, not least because of the amiable staff. They were so nice I actually looked forward to going in. I had treatment five days a week for just over six weeks.

On the last day of rads the radiation nurse said the skin might continue to burn after treatment finished. It did. My sister said that the side of the mastectomy looked like someone had squashed a red-hot iron on the breast and flattened it. Funny, it did.

On the next visit to the lymphoedema specialist I was given a compression sleeve. My arm was ever so slightly more swollen, he noted. I was to wear the sleeve until such swelling was reduced. It looked like one leg of a heavy pair of support nylons on my arm, of a colour you might call American Tan, of a denier that felt like it was in the high hundreds.

I texted a fellow mastectomy to tell her about my new medi-garment. 'Another thing to boost your sexuality,' she replied. Eventually I would be given a matching lymphoedema glove to wear, as my hand was swelling slightly. I soon got used to wearing both: they were just part of my 'new normal'.

'It's only when the treatment's all over that it hits,' other patients had said. My gut reaction was to get so busy I didn't have time to think. I was back writing and gigging with The Nualas again, first gig 23 March. We hadn't been onstage together since 26 November. I wore my lymphoedema sleeve on stage and we turned it into a gag:

SUE NUALA: I just want to congratulate Nuala on some charity work she did recently. She played the bodhrán for two and a half days non-stop for charity and raised €275.62 for her local donkey shelter.

MARIA NUALA: Thanks to Nuala, there's some very happy donkeys in The Liberties tonight.

ANNE NUALA: Thanks for that, girls. They just told me in Outpatients today that I should have some feeling back in the arm by September so I'm looking forward to grooming me some donkeys.

Cancer was over, more or less. There would be regular check-ups, gradually spaced from every four months for the first year to one a year for ten years to come, plus annual mammograms. Though the all-clear isn't given until five years without recurrence, the assessment seemed to be that I was cancer-free.

I'd been lucky, hadn't I?

The oncologist had told me to expect no periods ever again after chemotherapy, yet within seven months of the end of chemo they returned, with a vengeance, and was I ever delighted. I've talked to other women who saw the end of their periods through chemo as a good thing, albeit they were in their late forties and already mums. But I was bereft at the thought that mine had ended.

I felt so happy going back into Boots to buy the necessary, delighted to know again that I had an excuse for being grumpy, at least some of the time; that I could still feel this fundamental biological connection with the thirteen-year-old I had been when it had all begun, for another few years at least. 'You've the chance to start the huge family you always planned to start when you hit fifty,' friend Sue noted.

20. An End

As I write this conclusion I've just received word from the hospital that my breast reconstruction operation will take place within the next few months. This is such happy news. I shall be having a DIEP flap reconstruction. Skin and fat from the stomach will be removed and reconnected to the chest wall. The DIEP flap is the most complex reconstruction operation, so much so that many women offered reconstructions aren't given the option. The blood vessels to supply the fat tissue, the 'deep inferior epigastric perforators' (DIEP), have to be identified, carefully removed from the muscle of the stomach wall and reconnected to blood vessels sourced in the muscle of the chest wall. This removal and reconnection of blood vessels is a painstaking, time-sensitive operation, involving highly skilled micro-surgery. Post-operatively, the new breast will have to be checked every hour or two for the first forty-eight hours, to ensure the newly connected blood vessels supplying the former stomach tissue are 'taking'. It also entails the body being kept exceptionally warm for that length of time. It's major surgery, taking six to eight hours, with a hospital stay of at least a week, then a healing and recuperation period of two months.

The operation leaves a scar from hip to hip across the lower belly. Given the skin surface removed, from which the skin of the new breast is created, the external belly button is somewhat rejigged. There is a slight possibility this may not work. So I could be left with, if not the literal, then the metaphorical, stomach of an angel. Also, given the large ellipse of fat tissue that is removed, there's a tightening of the stomach. It takes some time before you can easily stand properly upright again. And, of course, you have to be careful with the new breast. The old wound will have been opened for the reconstruction, and there are many medical variables involved in the stomach tissue settling into its new role as living breast tissue and the dissected stomach skin adhering to remnants of the original breast surface on the chest. A bra support has to be worn 24/7 long afterwards. And then, in my case, as I'd had largish breasts, the other breast will have to be reduced, lifted and balanced to match. And then a new nipple created. And finally it's darker tone tattooed on, and the illusion of an areole tattooed around it. The process will spread over another year, at least.

Considering all of the above, the time, the cost, the intensity of aftercare and the level of surgical expertise involved, I found that I had to ask myself, 'Now, honestly, woman, is this really necessary? No matter the unconscionable official dishonesty that resulted in this nation state being in a pit of trans-generational debt, is what I'm being offered adding unnecessarily to it?' I'd already had the expensive life-saving treatment: chemotherapy, radiation, the mastectomy, not to mention all the attendant tests, medical support and follow-up appointments.

My brother, in his endless habitual foraging of second-hand bookshops, came across a seventies treatise by an African-American lesbian radical feminist. 'Thought you might be interested in this,' he said, handing me the slim old book in which the author railed angrily against much of what she'd experienced going through her breast-cancer treatment and mastectomy. Referring to the then innovative idea of breast reconstruction, she pontificated about it being concerned with 'the superficial aspects of women's breasts', and the justification for the operation being couched in 'the language of sexist pigs'. I had to take a long moment to work out was there truth in what she said: even to my long-attuned feminist ear, her ranting sounded passé, if understandable, of its time.

Breast reconstruction is offered now as a matter of course after mastectomy because women who have reconstructions have improved psychological and body-image outcomes. Simply, if something that evident on your body has been amputated, the opportunity to have it restored is considered a right in this neck of the woods. Especially since the art of reconstruction surgery has evolved to the point at which it can produce beautiful, heartening results. So, with all respect to my late lesbian radical-feminist sister, when I personally sat with the question of what was right for me, I found she was wrong.

Post-mastectomy, I could hardly bear to look at my naked body in the mirror. I gained a lot of weight post-treatment, my prosthesis became smaller than my natural breast; mostly I didn't wear it. I felt intensely unattractive, completely asexual. And though I didn't focus on that negativity, whenever I did think about it I felt a sorrow that I had no connection with my former confidence in my sexiness and all the physical joy that emanated from that happy corporeality. And, Goddamn it, I had to acknowledge that it bloody mattered! I couldn't be sustained by living in my head. One day it just clicked, and I went, 'It's definite – I need a new breast.'

Shortly after, at a party, a woman asked me how I was doing, and I said that I was looking forward to the reconstruction, the end of it all. And in she milled, telling me about the person she knew who had gone 'through the same as you', one breast lost to mastectomy and all the rest of it, but was she going for the reconstruction? Oh, no, because, that woman related to me, this lady's perspective was that the people who loved her loved her for herself, the way she was, so why bother? 'But she's a bit of a maverick,' the woman concluded.

Wow! Well, what could you say to that? 'Maverick, is it? What, you mean she's a bit of a runaway calf in a cowboy film? Holy God, I can't keep up with what you're implying at all, ya ould boot!'

The lesson: don't let anyone rain on your proposed new chest.

Deciding I wanted that operation was massively positive.

I have no fear of the post-operative pain, or wounds that will require protracted healing. I know from the mastectomy that they'll be there and then they'll be gone, I won't recall it, and a well body has the most extraordinary capacity for bouncing back. I know I'm lucky in that the public hospital I attend and the particular cosmetic surgeon I have been assigned are world class. And those few days being bedridden? No problem. At least I'll be set up for my favourite activity: sleep. However hot I get, whatever the number of surgical drains poking out above and below, whatever memories of cancer might be evoked, whatever the discomforts the procedure throws up, there's a heart-deep yearning to see the return of a mound of womanly flesh on this currently concavely flat chest. I know the new boobie won't have the former's sensitivity, but for the balance, the aesthetics, the personal sense of moving on and reconnection with my sexuality, it's essential for me.

Post-treatment, I had slipped back into the familiar black pits of despair, wanting-to-die territory. But what was different was that, given the exceptional medical care I had just received, I had renewed belief in formal systems of treatment and medication. I went to my doctor, and arranged for two things I'd said I'd never engage with again: psychotherapy and anti-depressant medication.

It might have been that determination to make it work, or my clarity about what I needed from each, or simply my decision to have faith in those processes – to believe that something medical could work for the mind, just as chemo-surgery-rads had worked on the body – but together they worked, are working.

I found my therapist through my GP. She chose someone she considered would match my personality. Rather than enter the 'you do all the talking, they the listening' dynamic I'd previously experienced, I told this new person I'd appreciate more of a dialogue. And so it has been. The long relationship we have now established is currently one of, if not *the*, most important touchstones in my life. There is never direct advice, but through weekly sounding out, and search for clarity, meaningfulness and best practice in daily engagement with life, it has been invaluable. It's been invaluable, for instance, in processing, and laying to rest, the cancer experience. Her therapy room has become a sacred place to share things – odd responses, senses of loss and difficult emotions – that are hard to tease out to oneself, and would be inappropriate to burden anyone else with. A secular confessional, you might say, but much more because it's not about guilt and forgiveness from on high, it's simply just about trying to be the most functional person you have the potential to be, addressed practically. About being your best self. About evolving knowledge of yourself, so your engagement with others, with the world, comes from a place of deep centredness – and so may you sow serenity where'er you go, ideally.

So now I couch this talk therapy, not, as my natural inclination would have it, as weakness or indulgence but as personal responsibility. It is my personal responsibility to be all right. This isn't about admitting to being weak, it's about being truly adult. As for medication, the practicalities of that matter are, after some trial and error, and balancing out past experiences: at the moment I take 60mg of Cymbalta (duloxetine) daily. It's an SNRI, serotonin and noradrenaline (norepinephrine) reuptake inhibitor, similar, but with slightly different action, to the Effexor I had previously taken.

Additionally, because the depressions have been lifelong recurrent, my GP suggested a referral to a psychiatrist. I hummed, hawed, dithered and then said, 'Yes.' I knew from my dexamethasone episode during chemo that I find the method of initial psychiatry assessment in the public teaching-hospital model difficult to deal with: one is, as a matter of course, assessed by students, and only then do you get access to the head honcho. Instinctively I feel psychological issues are too nuanced and complex to be dealt with in the same teaching-hospital manner as physical malady. Maybe I'm wrong. Whatever.

That's the way it is with the hospital I attend, and I figured it was worth accepting it to have access to the insight of a top-of-their-game consultant. There was a five-month wait, and appointment day happened to be my birthday. My medical present turned out to be an assessment by two massively novice novices, in a question-and-answer session sometimes verging on the blackest of black-comedy sketches. Then I got the face time with the consultant. And, after a slight contretemps over what I had just experienced in that long, odd Q&A, I established a good rapport with her. She made a, to me, surprise suggestion: to offset future serious recurrence I should consider taking a daily low dose of lithium, long term. I heard 'lithium' and thought, Whoa! I'm not a nut-job, am I? It seemed like a med too far, and one also, in my meagre understanding, that was indicated for psychiatric conditions far more severe than mine.

The consultant explained that lithium also has a tried and tested history of use in conjunction with anti-depressant medications as a treatment for recurrent major depressive disorder. Lithium's precise mechanism in this is not established, but it is regarded as a 'mood stabiliser' and it appears to enhance the brain serotonin level sustained by meds such as I'm already on. Because lithium works within a very tight window of concentration in the bloodstream, regular blood tests are required while the stable level is established. At the very least that was an issue for me because my veins are still fucked post-chemo and I simply couldn't endure regular spikes. And it will require more time, thought and research on my part, but at this point in my experience I find myself open to the notion, and respectful of the expertise, and good intentions, of the consultant who suggested it.

I relate all of the above in detail not in a deluded splurge of medical-information excitation but in an attempt to dispel some of the silent shame that always seems to cleave to the notion of taking psychiatric medication. 'If you were diabetic, would anyone question you needed insulin?' my local pharmacist asked.

I'd gone to him straight after the consultation, slightly in shock. 'Michael, lithium, me? What the ...?' Or words to that effect. From his perspective it represented a solid medical approach to addressing an illness issue.

I know the medicine route and formal medical diagnosis of depressive disorder comes with intense for-

and-against controversy, but leaving that aside may I just note that I have faith in formal/Western/whatever you want to call it medicine because of the incontrovertible excellence of it when it came to treating my cancer. So it seemed obvious to choose to have renewed openness to medication as a potential solution for my life-debilitating depression. But that doesn't take away the shame one feels in the admission that one requires such medication to function. And if I do go with the suggestion of ongoing low-dose lithium in the future, it's not that I'll be walking around with a T-shirt trumpeting 'I'M A LITHIUM CHICK. WHAT ABOUT YOU, LOSER?' I'm just saying that the shame isn't helpful, if you're facing similar decisions yourself.

There's the shame to deal with, and also, I've found, the intense resistance from those close – the mere name 'lithium', the mere notion that I might get involved with the hospital system to manage my mental health for ever; the fear I'm self-smearing my good name in inviting labelling by impartial medical officialdom; the fear of who knows what ramifications that might have in the future; the suggestion that I'm drawn to the idea because I've some sort of perverse desire to sustain engagement with hospital treatment, having grown so familiar with it over the long course of cancer treatment; the suggestion that it's weakness on my part, a childish desire to be taken care of, therefore a denigration of my mature adult self; the fear that it may change me, dull my personality, kill my creativity, deaden my connection to others. And not just all that! It's been suggested to me that I've never truly tried the long-term, pure-diet and regular, measured lifestyle route to address depression. 'Try that for a year, at least, then maybe think about lithium,' I've been told.

I hear what's been said, and I know, too, that dark place where everything stops, where you're dead without being dead, and making it truly so can seem like mere technicality. I cannot bear to be there again. And I absolutely know the SNRI medication I'm currently taking helps with staving off that place. So do I believe low-dose lithium could sustain this 'good place I'm in now' state for ever after? Possibly, because in going with medication I guess I'm accepting the 'chemical imbalance' theory of depression. And, yes, indeed, it may be that.

I recall having my first sense of deep bleakness when I was five years old and we were still in England. The sense is still clear in memory: the little dress I was wearing, our Manchester kitchen, and this gloom from nowhere descending. Ostensibly everything was happy then, so is the gloom dispositional, genetically set in the brain mechanics Fate bequeathed me? Moving to Ireland, months later, circumstances coalesced to breed misery, so is the gloom situational, an unavoidable consequence of the protracted unhappy circumstance Fate flung at me?

Maybe it's a mushing of both – and there's that other old chestnut in the mix: transgenerational issues. 'Death before dishonour' is the most emotional thing I ever heard my paternal grandmother say, a wrinkled old woman I knew a few years before her death. Nothing in the realm of a hug would ever have occurred to her – I found her instinctive coldness interesting, even as a child. I never knew my paternal grandfather but, by all accounts, he was an extraordinary, rather genius man and a sufferer of the gloom. I garnered this from snatched wisps of information: there was mostly silence on family history when I was growing up. Latterly I came to wonder did he not suffer somewhat from what we would now term post-traumatic stress disorder, after his endeavours for a free Ireland? I wondered that again when I came across his detailed account of his experiences, stored in the Irish Bureau of Military History.

There is so much we come from of which we have little clue; so much driving us it could drive us mad to think too hard on it. The chemical soup in the brain; the complex folds of its mass; the brain and body tincture of instinct, the brain and body memory of formative experience, of family, cultural and race history. And our will in it all, telling us go on, you will, you will, you will, and us having to believe, day to day, that that's what it's all about, really, even as we know it's not.

For much of my life, when I thought of the past, of the childhood in Sligo, I felt a ferocious anger – about the heap of rancid memory and emotion it had left, and the hole, too, where a sense of rootedness and home could have been. If I thought about it, it seemed the shame emitted from those years had seeped over everything that succeeded. The claws of those feelings of shame that had stalked me since my childhood had pushed back other people, who, being close, might have exploded life into positivity. It seemed those claws had ripped them up any time a sense of being all right took root, destroying any possibility of 'normality' or happiness. There was blame in all this, useless, immature blame, which felt it belonged with the adults of back then.

I never spoke with, hardly ever saw, my father. I hadn't returned to his place in years. And then, after all, I did. With my sister Una, in her ancient red Nissan Micra, with her scruffy rescue dog, Patch. And oddly, as we drove west the sickening feeling that always seeped into me as the landscape became the yellow-green, hedge-conglomerated unfolding of Connaught, and the bit of Sligo where we were raised, was gone.

After we'd checked into a local hotel, our first stop wasn't visiting, but a trip to the bog. The dog dashed up and down the rough old track roads, delighted with rural freedoms. The sky was doing all sorts, heavy with blue cloud and light with white, cracks splaying rays of wane sunlight between, plops of cold rain intermittent. Along the track roads, blackened whin-bush stalks showed where there'd been old fire, and pale yellow grasses bunched along and across the rutted land, like quiffs of thick wild hair. Deep black splits in the land showed the depth of ancient peat beneath the surface. 'Is it something our memories put onto this that make it feel so heavy?' I asked Una. And she said she didn't know: it was hard to see it like a hiking German or some such with touristic eyes might.

Was that lonely soul-opening feeling, which seemed to seep in with the trickle of hidden streams, or whine on the cold breeze whipping across the flat banks, universal? Beyond just our history, was it something in the place itself that made the mind drift always from the now to what had previously passed over?

I looked to the particular stretch of banks we had worked summers, every year, and felt we were still, and would always be, there: my brother, sister and I, children in wellies, bent, clumping turf together, imagining the footings we built were magical kingdoms that would fill with fairies once we left for the day – the emptiness between bleak sky and harsh, silent land demanding the mind rush in with imaginings to colour it with something Goddamn lovelier, or just tantalisingly other. And is that part-genesis of the Irish imagination, the grasp for something more than the landscape starkness on offer, the fantasy of spellbinding peoples beneath the ground, of banshees and changelings, and hares that were bold hussies under their mere bland rabbity exteriors? That led my siblings and I not just to seek solace but our very livelihoods, our lives' work, in the arena of the madey-up.

There was a chat with my father later in a pub, in the town, on a night hopping with St Patrick's Day celebration. It was almost as if there had never been any issue, and him, as is his wont, talking about distant things. About history older than ours: my grandfather narrowly escaping the Black and Tans, who had wheeled their bicycles right into the kitchen of the house one Sunday morning, looking for him, demanding of my grandmother that they'd heard he came back of a Sunday, and her fobbing them off because it happened he wasn't there. Them being intent on blue murder, and her, phenomenally brave woman, somehow managing to leave a signal that could be seen from outside that would tell my grandfather to get away if he happened back. 'Those people made some sacrifices,' my dad said, meaning his father, his mother, others who'd fought for Irish Independence. He asked me that we look after the old house when he was gone, for him.

I snorted. 'But it's falling down.'

'It's not,' he said. 'There's some history there. Look after it is all I'm asking.' I could only laugh at the madness of the request in the context of everything else. It revealed something that might later be processed as understanding.

It was only when I got thankfully back to Dublin the next day, having driven home with Una and the dog, that I realised every shred of old anger was gone. Finally, oddly, and about finally time, I felt like I wasn't still haunted and fraught by the shadow of those old childhood feelings.

That, feckin' conveniently for the resolution of this book, there came about a big capital R for resolution in my own head.

That resolution I see as wholly thanks to cancer: I had secretly embraced the disease when I was diagnosed, silently delighted I might have been handed an easy exit from life. Then a structure of medical care kicked in that was so dense with new experience, orchestrated by a cast of such interesting professional people, with such liveliness of endeavour, in such a particularly well-run hospital, that I felt distracted back into the dynamics of being alive. But not just distracted – embraced by the driving ethos beneath the whole process: that life is worth cherishing, preserving, fighting for, no question, no ambiguity. That hospital was a temple to belief in the absolute preciousness of life, its daily activity a ceremony to honour that faith. Because of cancer, I was swept into a system that said, 'Your life is worth living.' To be part of it was to experience an unconditional reflection of worth. In that regard, I tend to see the cancer as a gift, and the curing of it not just as life-saving, but the most deeply life-changing experience I've had.

What I'm left with is a sense of gratitude, for the people I met through cancer, for the experiences that opened up with cancer, for each day that dawns after cancer – not to mention the beautiful new breasts, one re-created, one lifted and reduced to match, that I'll be sporting thanks to cancer. To reduce those sentiments to the core or, shall we say, the nipple of the matter, I feel I was saved by breast cancer.

The line that comes to mind in conclusion is from the medieval German mystic Meister Eckhart:

If there's only one prayer you ever say in your entire life, let it be 'thank you'...

With the performer's addendum I've spoken zillions of times exiting stage: 'And good night.'

Leabharlanna Poiblí Chathair Bhaile Átha Cliath
Dublin City Public Libraries

Acknowledgments

Gratitude to: Una and Kevin for always being there.

All the so many family, friends, correspondents and acquaintances – personal, professional and medical – for myriad sustaining kindnesses: Briefly, not exhaustively, but most especially Brian Finnegan for encouraging me to keep going, when twice I was about to throw in the towel in this endeavour. Larissa Kouznetsova, Antoinette Azzurro and Ann-Marie Gilkes for journeys made when I was ill, not to mention most helpful reader notes. Carmel Keary and Patricia Dunne, for support, and sharing previous experiences of breast cancer; in that, too, thanks to Dympna Watson of Europa Donna Ireland. Libby McCormack and Anna Rodgers for making the documentary that preceded the writing of this book, and RTÉ for their tremendous support of that project. Also, Sinead Ryan and Joanne Byrne. My dear sister-in-law Tracy Rennie, and forever-comedy-chums Michelle Read and Susan Collins.

All at The Tyrone Guthrie Centre, as always, for the

welcome, and heavenly place to work.

My editor Ciara Considine, all at Hachette Ireland, and my agent, John Saddler. Associated Press (Ireland) for permission to use material from my column in *The Irish Mail on Sunday*, in particular, thanks to Sharon Miney, Aileen Doherty and Sebastian Hamilton.

Finally, deepest gratitude to St James' Hospital, Dublin, for everything and in remembrance of my kind, exceptional radiologist, the late Professor Donal Hollywood.

The witness statement of my grandfather is available online at www.bureauofmilitaryhistory.ie; click on 'Index of Witnesses', search 'Charles Gildea'.

About the Author

Anne Gildea is a Dublin-based writer and performer. In a varied career, she has toured internationally with her all-girl comedic songster group The Nualas; has written and performed comedy material for radio and television for both RTÉ in Ireland and the BBC in the UK; has worked as a solo stage comedienne and is a published novelist. She is a weekly columnist with *The Irish Mail on Sunday*.